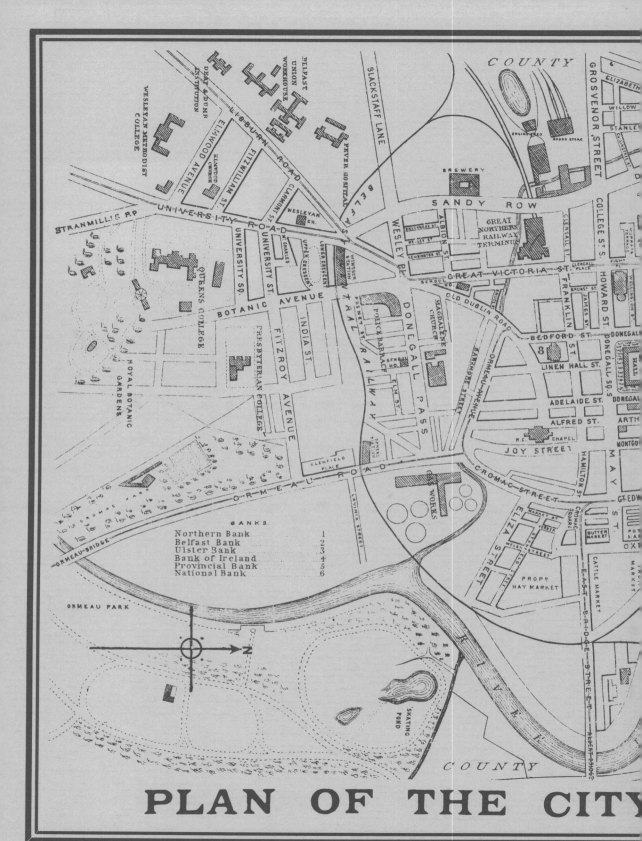

PLAN OF THE CITY

BANKS.

Northern Bank	1
Belfast Bank	2
Ulster Bank	3
Bank of Ireland	4
Provincial Bank	5
National Bank	6

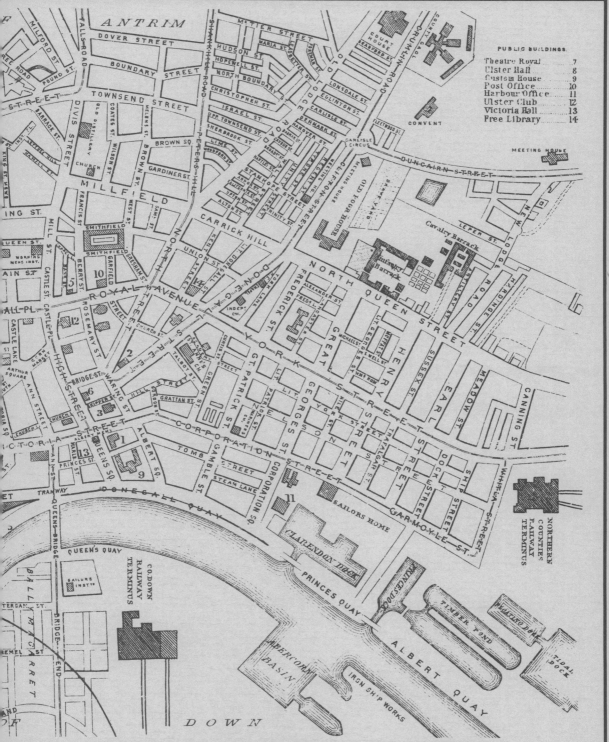

OF BELFAST 1897

BUILDINGS OF BELFAST

1700—1914

C. E. B. BRETT

BUILDINGS OF BELFAST

1700—1914

Revised edition 1985

FRIAR'S BUSH PRESS
24 College Park Avenue
Belfast 7

© C. E. B. Brett 1967
First published by Weidenfeld and Nicolson
London, 1967

Second impression 1969

This revised edition Friar's Bush Press
Belfast, 1985

ISBN 0 946872 02 3

Typeface: English
Typesetting: Compuset, Lisburn Road, Belfast
Screen negatives: Reprographics, Dublin Road, Belfast
Printing: Universities Press, Alanbrooke Road, Belfast
Designer: Spring Graphics, Saintfield

CONTENTS

LIST OF PLATES

INTRODUCTION

to the revised edition

In the years since 1966, the architectural character of Belfast has changed utterly: and not for the better. It has been a sobering experience to re-perambulate its streets (or such of them as still exist) carrying the same notebook in which I started work more than a quarter-century ago, on the first of January, 1959, on the first edition of this book. Then, and still at the time of publication, Belfast was (as I wrote) "a very individual city, with a pronounced character all its own"; a character made up of an uncommon combination of Georgian, low and high Victorian, and Edwardian, buildings, with—at any rate in the city centre—only a tolerable sprinkling of incongruous later ones.

In fact, a surprising number of the best individual buildings recorded in 1966 are still there; it is their surroundings rather than themselves which have mostly deteriorated. But the overall effect has nonetheless been horrifying.

Four principal causes have contributed to this. Three of them—the property boom of the 'sixties and early 'seventies; the inexorable processes of inner-city decay; and the constant growth in the demands for space of cars, vans, lorries, containers, and juggernauts—have, in varying degrees, exerted similar pressures on almost every other city in the western world. The fourth cause, the so-called 'Troubles' of Ulster, has been purely local. And in my view the compound fractures so inflicted have been aggravated by the unsympathetic fashions of the day amongst architects, engineers, and town planners.

The property boom, which lasted from the mid-sixties until the mid-seventies, struck all too damagingly at the dignified mercantile heart of Victorian and Edwardian Belfast. Many fine buildings were lost, and many greatly inferior ones were substituted for them. Few of the new buildings, even when tolerably good in themselves, were in scale or sympathy with their neighbours; although in this respect there has been some improvement in the eighties. Happily, many office blocks of this period are already suffering from the defects of their shoddiness, and, it may reasonably be hoped, will fall down soon.

There is no lack of egregious examples: one of the most striking was the destruction of the very fine warehouse block in Bedford Street (see plate 30) and its lesser but worthy neighbours in Franklin Street and James Street South, despite loud cries of protest, to make way for the 23-storey Windsor House. This was doubly tragic: for an insurance company had been found, able and willing to restore and modernise the existing buildings, until deterred by the unrest in the city; moreover, it is now widely acknowledged to have been a grave mistake to have allowed so exceptionally tall a building to over-shadow the City Hall and the heart of the city.

Another case where developers and bombers between them brought about disaster was the Ulster Club in Castle Place, an imposing building by Sir Charles Lanyon. After it had been vacated by the clubmen, it lay vacant for many months, indeed years, and suffered bomb damage which was allowed to go unrepaired; on my last visit to it, in company with Philip Goodhart (then minister at the Department of the Environment), whom I still hoped to persuade to refuse consent for demolition, we had both to wear gum-boots even in the ground-floor rooms, so deep was the litter of soaked plaster and reeking pigeon-dung which, along with wet rot everywhere, had resulted from holes in the roof and broken windows left unmended. Alas, even I was forced to conclude that it was a hopeless case for restoration and it seemed not right to demand a replica.

The record of public bodies in the field of office design is no more creditable than that of the private developers: Churchill House, River House, Telephone House, the Post Office slab fronting Donegall Quay, the Ministry of Commerce block in Chichester Street: none of these is a loved or loveable ornament to the landscape. Most of the new office-blocks, public or private, are in the faceless international style, and could be anywhere in the world: whereas the banks, warehouses and offices they replaced were richly carved and detailed in an individual and inimitable style more characteristic of Belfast than of any other city.

The population of the city has fallen quite sharply from a peak of 443,000 in 1951 to an estimated figure, at the date of writing, of 305,000, notwithstanding the boundary extension of 1971. In some ways this fall of well over 25% in the inhabitants of a formerly greatly overcrowded city has been a good thing, though of course it has brought some awkward problems in its wake. What brought it about? Partly it has been due to slum clearance, euphemistically called 'redevelopment', and the far higher space standards required for the replacement dwellings. Partly it has been due to a contraction in the traditional inner-city industries, combined with the establishment of new industrial estates in a twenty-five-mile ring all around the city; followed by a general recession affecting all manufacturing. Partly it has been due to the flight of warehousing and wholesaling to the outskirts, because of the difficulty of handling large container loads in congested streets and loading-bays. Partly it has been due to changes (very regrettable ones, many people feel) in the pattern of shopping: the closure not only of the hundreds of small uneconomic back-street shops, but also of traditional general or specialist emporiums in the city centre (such as Robb's, Arnott's, Robinson & Cleaver's, the Bank Buildings); and the growth of shopping centres, served by acre upon acre of car-parks, around the periphery. Partly it has been due to the natural wish of young householders to bring up their families in pleasanter surroundings than the old narrow streets, their still narrower back alleys, and their overcrowded parks and playgrounds; not to mention the vandalism and violence endemic in so many districts.

As the human population has dwindled, so the pressures of road traffic and the demands for parking have increased. It must be acknowledged, however ruefully, that action had to be taken if the whole city was not quickly to become clogged up. In the late 1960's, ambitious road plans, involving extensive demolition, were drawn up. There was, in particular, much debate on the scheme for a six-lane Urban Motorway, to cut a broad swathe right through the northern sections of the inner city. Several alternative routes were canvassed; one political party came up with a particularly ingenious route which would have meant the demolition of the headquarters of all its rivals! In the end, the original scheme was abandoned on grounds mostly of its phenomenal cost; and the Westlink, a comparatively narrow four-lane roadway, in parts sunken, without hard shoulders or extravagant landscaping (but also without separation of levels at several busy junctions) was built instead.

The combined effect of the opening of this new road, and the closing to through traffic (for security reasons) of the former main axis of the city through Donegall Place and Royal Avenue, has wrought the single largest change from any cause in the character and structure of Belfast. The inner and outer roadways (still far from complete) which have accompanied it have had almost equally devastating effects. Vast dreary car-parks, still inadequate to the demand as they are, have finally broken up the city's streetscape and pattern.

This is not all loss, of course; traffic jams and parking problems in Belfast are very much less severe than those in Dublin, where (rightly or wrongly) much less attempt has been made to tame the motor-car. But unhappily, however technically proficient they may be, roads engineers seem to be rather an insensitive body of men. Countless good buildings, and a few exceptionally fine ones, have been swept away; wide acres of tarmac and cement, retaining walls, ugly street furniture, railings and the all-pervading invasion of space-left-over, have replaced a formerly dignified and coherent townscape with a kind of vast, straggling, unworthy no-man's land.

Many visitors to Belfast have been appalled by the wide acres of wasteland and devastation, which they have been too hasty in attributing entirely to the Troubles. Yet the Troubles have caused damage enough. The bombing campaigns, at their worst in 1970-73 but flaring up again from time to time ever since, have been for the most part aimed at "economic targets"—warehouses, shops, public-houses, offices; or at public buildings; or premises used by the police or army. In some instances the targets have been very deliberately selected, but probably more often the sites have been chosen just so as to inflict a maximum of damage. Great quantities of explosives have been used, often in car-bombs. It is not to be overlooked that, for every building actually destroyed, very many others—within a radius as great as a quarter of a mile—may suffer serious injury. Window-sashes, doors, slates, skylights, roof-timbers, chimneys, have often been destroyed, over a wide area, and by no means always replaced. Incendiaries and fire-bombs have had on the whole slightly less extensive effects, though a fire may spread from the building attacked to its neighbours; and gutted buildings are seldom capable of reconstruction.

In the residential parts of the city, though indeed bomb-damage and fire-damage have not been unknown (as witness the burning of whole terraces at Bombay Street in 1969 and Farringdon Gardens in 1971), the pattern of damage has been somewhat different. Here, rioting, street-fighting, barricades, and gunfire between the "defenders" of adjacent but mutually hostile areas, have led to massive population movements: the first wave in the autumn of 1969, the second in the summer of 1971. Since then, each community has retreated into its own territory, and derelict strips of uninhabitable no-man's land mark the dividing-lines between the zones.

In physical terms, the visible consequences of this unrest have been striking: but they have also changed progressively over the troubled years. At quite an early stage, the whole central shopping area of the City was ringed with steel railings and security gates, of great ugliness, designed to exclude the bombers. (It is a remarkable fact that these railings followed almost exactly the line of the long-demolished 17th century town ramparts). The area within the barriers became an at first involuntary, but later a popular and highly successful, large-scale pedestrian precinct. Metal barrels or concrete tubs filled with cement were placed around likely targets so as to make impossible the near approach of car-bombers. Booms, locked at night, were placed across the roads at the principal crossing points between the territory of one faction and the other. Windows were first criss-crossed with adhesive tape, then treated with shatter-proof film; or covered in steel grilles; or, following the invention of the grille-bomb using a butcher's double hook, covered altogether in steel plate. In the working class streets, screens of corrugated iron were at an early stage erected by the army along some of the most violent boundaries of confrontation, and wryly christened "Peace Lines". (It is a remarkable fact that the barrier between the Falls and Shankill Roads follows, to within a few inches, the dividing line recorded by the Commission of Inquiry into the Belfast riots of 1886.) Police stations and army posts in central and outer areas alike were increasingly heavily fortified with sandbags, tall wire-mesh screens, "sangars", pill-boxes, humps in the roadway outside, and chicanes.

To an astonishing extent, the city has now assimilated, and even come to take for granted, these extraordinary adjuncts to urban life as it is mostly lived elsewhere. The railings and security gates have been 'prettified': they have today something of the look of ornamental garden wrought-iron gates. The tubs and barrels have largely been replaced by elegant cast-iron bollards with an ornamental sea-horse (from the city's coat of arms) picked out in a contrasting colour. The peace lines have been rebuilt in brick, sometimes with decorative insets and graffito repellent. (Incidentally, the M1 Motorway and Westlink roadway serve as another rough and ready peace line along some parts of their length). Pill-boxes are fetchingly disguised as *cottages ornées*; new police stations are designed to be defensible in the most tasteful way possible. The pedestrianisation of the city centre has proved a blessing in disguise; the suspicious shopkeepers would never before have agreed to it, but now the lunch-time crowds in Ann Street, Cornmarket, Castle Lane and Donegall Place on sunny days have brought back prosperity from the shopping centres of the outer suburbs. There is a sort of grim realism about the design of new buildings of every kind, including public and private houses: security considerations are seldom left altogether out of account: but then, security from robbers and vandals is a material consideration elsewhere, too.

In all this, a factor often overlooked, but of inestimable importance, has been the code of compensation for malicious injury to property. Although there has never been any comparable system in Britain in peace time (the War Damage Acts were very similar), and though few other countries have any comparable code, provisions of this kind have been required in Ireland off and on ever since the 17th century. The compensation has not been lavish, especially in a time of inflation, but it has been adequate. There has been much laudable rebuilding, though the tricky concept of 'betterment' has sometimes resulted in the substitution of a cheap and functional new building for a run-down if elegant old one. In other cases, especially in the sensitive University area of the City, exact replicas of bombed buildings (externally at any rate) have been reconstructed; which has given rise to some debate on the point of principle. My own view is that, as in bomb-damaged cities elsewhere such as Leningrad and Budapest, this is not only justifiable, it is the only correct answer, where the buildings are of intrinsic merit as elements in the townscape, or important as parts of a larger terrace or group.

The redevelopment of the crowded streets of red-brick kitchen and parlour houses has also given rise to controversy. Some have argued that the retention of existing communities is more important than the renewal of these tiny and, often, jerry-built homes. Some conservationists have argued, not without force, that redevelopment has completely altered the character of the city; and that even the smallest houses should still be repaired and modernised for single people, rather than replaced. For my part, I take the contrary view, and have done all in my power to secure the provision of better and larger family houses in place of those which, as it seems to me, are worn out and incapable of providing for the needs of the parents and children of the future. Time will show which view is right; in the meanwhile, I can at least plead consistency: for in 1966 I wrote:

"I am not a wholesale preservationist; Belfast greatly needs replanning and redevelopment. An enormous proportion especially of its dwelling-houses are worn out and need replacement."

I stand by those sentiments.

But having said this, I hold no brief for the high-rise blocks, towers and slabs which during the late 1960's and '70s were as popular amongst planners and architects for housing as they were for offices (and even hospitals). Tall blocks *can* work (at any rate, so long as the lifts work) in some places, and for some kinds of tenants, however visually intrusive they may be. But they will not work for high-density communities with many children and adolescents; especially in a time of recession and unemployment; more especially where vandalism, hooliganism, and civil unrest are endemic. Yet the planners should not be called upon to bear the entire blame for developments such as the now-demolished 'Weetabix' flats (so called from their resemblance to breakfast-cereal packets) on the Shankill Road, or the notorious Divis flats on the Falls Road. The territorial imperative played its part: and some communities insisted—usually at the instigation of their clerical or political leaders (or misleaders)—on the entire populace being rehoused within the same parish or electoral ward, despite the evident impossibility of doing so without building upwards. Those same communities should not now be too quick to blame others.

Yet it is curious that the extremes of verticality, and also of horizontality, should have taken such a grip of architectural fashion: and that in-between buildings of three, four or five storeys are now both scarce and unpopular. The merchant and the shopkeeper alike now seem to favour great echoing single-storey hangars; each would be scandalised by any suggestion that he should return to the custom of his forebears, and live above the shop or counting-house; he much prefers his bungalow, or ranch-house, or his Spanish patio. The designers and users of schools, factories, leisure centres, clinics, old peoples' homes, all want them to be on one or at most two floors. Even the tenant or buyer of a new house is no longer content to climb more than one flight of stairs if he can help it: so that the excellent old-fashioned three- or four-storeyed terrace houses of the past (admittedly expensive to heat, carpet and furnish) are quite out of fashion.

This trend has caused much damage to the appearance of the city. Georgian, Victorian and Edwardian Belfast derived its character to a great extent from the seemly terraces which lined all its streets and radial roads: fine tall buildings in or near the centre, slightly less tall ones further out, but still coherent and dignified on frontages such as those of University Road, the Antrim Road, the Ormeau Road. Not only do people not want to live in tall houses like these today, they do not much want to live facing the noise, smells, vibration and pollution generated by heavy traffic on the main roads. (Horses were smelly, carts and carriages were noisy, and traffic accidents not infrequent, a century ago; but that is by the way). So what is to be built along these road frontages? No so-called barrier block yet designed is visually satisfactory. The Housing Executive has made valiant efforts to develop a new formula, particularly the three-storey dwellings it has built on the Antrim Road and the Donegall Pass; but it is only in rare cases that the commercial frontages to main roads fall within the remit of the Executive. Unless means can be found of providing suitably scaled and proportioned buildings to front onto the main roads of the city (not to mention the Westlink), the appearance, character and integrity of Belfast will continue to degenerate as they have done over the past two decades.

In 1966, I remarked that Belfast was then a grossly overcrowded city, with little greenery and far too little open space. That state of affairs has changed: with the fall in the population, especially in Protestant areas, there is now a great deal more breathing-room and open space, save in the overcrowded enclaves (such as Falls Road and New Lodge) where Roman Catholic families took refuge in the period when the Troubles were at their worst. Too much is still wasteland, and too much is unlovely car- and lorry-parking space. Despite the very considerable efforts of the municipal parks department, vandalism is endemic, and 'hard' landscaping has better chances of survival than lawns, shrubs or trees. Still, a great many new small parks or gardens have been laid out, trees and bushes have been planted in the pavements of inner-city streets and along the verges of the new through roads: and great pertinacity in replacing vandalised stumps over and over again is beginning to show results. But mindless vandalism remains a problem of frightening proportions. Graffiti, wall-paintings, and the outward symbols of sectarianism have become both commoner and, by far, more offensive. Despite repeated efforts to clean up the city, it seems to a great extent to have lost its former pride in itself. This is well exemplified in the older cemeteries: Clifton Street burial-ground, where many of the most distinguished citizens of past generations were laid to rest in leafy and dignified surroundings, is in a quite horrifying state. Crow-bars, sledge-hammers, and ropes must have been needed for much of the destruction; even the tombs of Mary Ann McCracken, of Dr. Drennan, of Marcus Ward, of John Ritchie (first shipbuilder of Belfast) are not spared swastikas, "Black Sabbath", "Satan", "Sid Vicious", and "Punk" in aerosol lettering; two of the most lurid current graffiti at the time of writing are "Harry Wylie sniffed here" and "Death, we're back".

The number of drinking clubs, leisure centres, Chinese take-aways, and playing-fields has increased sharply. The number of public-houses, cinemas, and corner shops has decreased equally sharply. The number of churches has remained roughly constant—a few have been demolished, a few new ones have been built; but congregations have been dwindling, especially in or near the city centre, as a result more of the shifting population than of any evident diminution in religiosity. The future of a number of fine Georgian and Victorian church buildings must now be in doubt.

So far, I have had to paint a sombre picture. The first edition of this book was compiled and published only just in the nick of time: for the major changes in the face and character of Belfast, and the progressive deterioration to which I have referred, date from the traumatic years 1968 and 1969; and all that stemmed from the unhappy events of those years. Nevertheless, not all has been loss, and there is a happier side also to the recent history of the buildings of the city.

I recorded in 1966 that my book represented a venture into wholly unexplored territory. It has been gratifying, and a considerable relief, that not many errors of fact or attribution have come to light in what was very much a pioneering work. But it has been more than gratifying to watch a whole new generation of architectural historians, far better qualified and far more professional than I could ever hope to be, working in the field. Of course, Irish architectural history has itself been a growth industry over the past fifteen years or so. The rise in popularity of local history societies, and the impressive improvement in the quality of their publications, has also been remarkable. Particularly important contributions to the elucidation of the history of the buildings of Belfast have been made by Hugh Dixon; David Evans; Paul Larmour; Brian Walker; Peter Rankin; Marcus Patton; and Alistair Rowan. There is still no Pevsner volume, still no Victoria County History, still no adequate published statutory list for Belfast. But, whereas in 1966 there was not a single volume, there are now a considerable number of publications throwing light on the subject: and a select bibliography of those primarily concerned with the city's buildings (excluding books on other subjects, though with architectural overtones) will be found at page

There has been a corresponding shift in public opinion, largely due to the formation in 1967 of the Ulster Architectural Heritage Society as an all-purpose pressure group for architectural conservation throughout the nine counties of Ulster. By 1973, after the publication of the first handful in a series of free-lance surveys and lists of buildings of its own, it had shamed Government into setting up an Historic Buildings Council for Northern Ireland, with the functions of listing, administering grant aid, and identifying and declaring Conservation areas. Despite its very late start, and despite severe restrictions on the money and manpower made available to it, the Council has made a more than creditable beginning, as recorded in its 1985 publication *Taken for Granted*. It must be said that listing within the boundaries of Belfast remains far from complete; and, when a major building such as James Owen's General Post Office comes under threat, the arguments of the property speculator still tend to prevail.

Nonetheless, there have been many major achievements. The restoration and refurbishment, by the Arts Council, of the Grand Opera House; the restoration by the National Trust, jointly with Bass (Ireland) Ltd., of the Crown Bar; the painstaking renewal of the Palm House in the Botanic Gardens by Belfast City Council, as its contribution to European Architectural Heritage Year; the conversion of Elmwood Presbyterian church to a lecture and concert hall by the Queen's University; the restoration of an entire terrace of late Georgian houses in Joy Street by the Northern Ireland Housing Executive; the similar restoration of a terrace in Camden Street by the HEARTH housing association; most recently, the remarkably polished conversion by Marks & Spencer PLC of the old Richardson Sons & Owden's warehouse to an extension of their store; these have all been triumphs. Many other and lesser schemes, much stone-cleaning and repainting (in many but not all cases with the assistance of one or another category of grant) have made a very positive contribution to the architectural health of the city.

Here two tributes will not be out of place. First, to the successive ministers of all parties who, since the inception of direct rule, have shown a sympathetic understanding, and a willingness to invest money in the fabric, of Belfast, which, it must be said, compare favourably with the general apathy of most of their predecessors. Second, to those members of the architectural profession who have set to with a will to learn the arts of restoration and rehabilitation, previously not in great demand. Some of them have devoted great skill, commitment and sensitivity to the task. It is sad that Belfast has produced no really major architect in this century: at any rate, none whose name springs to mind so readily as the names of Lanyon, Lynn, and Barre. There is no original work in Belfast by either of the two leading living Irish architects, Michael Scott and Liam McCormick. There is little to attract the educated tourist seeking examples of first-rate work by architects from elsewhere—with the possible exception of Yorke, Rosenberg and Mardall's Synagogue in the Somerton Road, arguably the most distinguished work of modern architecture in the city.

However, I must not stray into territory where, by my own confession, I am incompetent to pass judgement: by reason of my unfortunate inability adequately to discount the influence of passing fashion on my judgements of the work of the past fifty years. It would have been nice to have taken the opportunity of this new edition to bring my closing date forward, if not to 1985, at any rate to 1939; but after careful cogitation, I decided against doing so; and will leave the field clear for some other author more in sympathy with the styles and schools of the last half-century than am I.

This book is a 'new' edition in the sense that I have tried, in the case of every building mentioned in 1966, to record the fact if it has gone up in the world, come down in the world, or actually disappeared, between December 1966 and May 1985. The text of the original edition remains intact; a few misprints and slips have been corrected; nothing else has been omitted, deleted, or rephrased, except in the captions to the illustrations; all the new information has been incorporated into footnotes. The references have also now been incorporated into the footnotes in order to avoid the complication of a double system of numbering. The distribution of stars and crossed swords remains unchanged. The Index has been revised only so far as was necessary. I have made no attempt to remedy omissions:

although during the past eighteen years, I have discovered, or revised my view of, a number of interesting and deserving buildings which were not mentioned. I had been given a strict limit on length by my original publishers, no bad discipline; and as I plainly stated in my preface, I tried to deal with every building of importance within the central area, but only with outstanding representative buildings in the suburbs and outskirts. It was very hard to decide whether to make changes in the illustrations themselves: in fact, they have been reproduced exactly as before, in some cases with up-dated captions. Had new illustrations been substituted for the original ones, then this would have become a new book, not a new edition; and if new illustrations had been added rather than substituted, then this would have become a far more expensive book. It has been out of print for a good many years; I can but hope that its renewed availability, and the amount of new material now added, one way or another, will justify the decision to republish it.

How far, in fact, have my tastes changed, my opinions altered, over the years since I compiled the first edition of this book? Not a great deal. I was far too sparing with my awards of three stars, two, or one, to buildings I admired; for I was very much afraid of appearing to overstate my case, and so antagonising those in authority. Certainly I should sprinkle my stars amongst the surviving buildings with a much more generous hand today. I have come to have an increasing admiration for the styles of the High Victorian period; also those of the Edwardians and the practitioners of Art Nouveau; but then that is hardly surprising, for so much important work has been published in these fields since 1966. I have also come to feel more strongly than ever about the merit of the Irish school of sculptors and stone-carvers. It is a shame that so much good work has been contemptuously swept away; a shame that there is so little place for new sculpture in the buildings of the present day. Almost alone, the Ulster Bank and its architect, Tony Houston, deserve a compliment for commissioning the two splendid figures at Shaftesbury Square—christened by my late dear friend, James Boyce, Draught and Overdraft—from Elizabeth Frink: even if they are attached to a building which is, itself, regrettably mediocre; and even if she is in no sense an Irish sculptor.

One great fallacy into which too many architectural historians are tempted to plunge, and which afflicts also the planners and administrators of Belfast, is the belief that a building of historical or architectural significance can be viewed in isolation from its surroundings. In a city with so peculiar a recent history as Belfast, this is an especial temptation. It really is not much more than winning half the battle to preserve individual buildings, if this takes place amidst surroundings which are utterly incongruous. It is of the utmost importance that in places such as College Square; University Road; Royal Avenue; the vicinity of St Malachy's church, or of the City Hall; every new candidate must be quizzed mercilessly: and that those which do not come up to the appropriate standard of urbanity be black-balled. The case for Conservation Area treatment in various parts of the city grows stronger day by day; as also, the need for the planners to look at new proposals in context, not in isolation.

In preparing this new edition, I must gratefully acknowledge the generous help and support in particular of Hugh Dixon, who has unstintingly made available his stores of knowledge and notes; of Sally Lowry, my secretary; Robin Harrison of the Northern Ireland Housing Executive; and, for the illustrations, Patrick Rossmore, the Irish Architectural Archive in Dublin, Alistair Rowan and Edward McParland; Dr. W. A. Maguire and the Ulster Museum; Leslie Stuart; and all those (individually noted in the list of plates) who allowed me to make use of their pictures. I owe thanks also to John Gray and Gerry Healey, and the staff, of the ever invaluable Belfast Linen Hall Library; and to the very many individuals, who, over the years, have courteously provided helpful information or access to their buildings.

June 1985   C. E. B. B.

PREFACE

Belfast is a very individual city, with a pronounced character all its own. Its flavour is quite different from that of Dublin, or Liverpool, or Cork, or Glasgow. Superficial observers often see only the Black City, capital of the Black North, gloomy, smoke-shrouded, rain-sodden. But it is much more than an Irish Ashton-under-Lyne. The sun does shine; the smoke is blown away to sea; the city is full of vigorous architecture and robust detailing. And though, as a community, it lives its life in a manner always idiosyncratic and sometimes outrageous, Belfast is never in any circumstances a dull or boring place to live.[1] It is a city which can provoke in its citizens a mixture of exasperation and affection.

The city is built on a saucer of flat ground at the head of Belfast Lough. To the east lies the Irish Sea, with Ailsa Craig on the horizon; to the west, the valley of the River Lagan. To the south are the Castlereagh hills; to the north, the higher slopes of the Antrim escarpment, the most prominent peak the Cave Hill, visible from all parts of the city through a screen of spires, chimneys, lift-shafts, water-tanks, gasometers, domes and blocks of flats.

There is no local building stone of merit; the gritty granite of the Mourne Mountains is not well suited to the needs of architecture. Most of the stone buildings of Belfast are of imported Scottish sandstone. There are no good local slate-quarries. Brick-clay there is; many of the hollows and valleys of the city's streets mark the worked-out clay-pits. The abundant forests which used to cover Ulster, and in which the original inhabitants took shelter from the Scottish and English settlers in the seventeenth century, have long since disappeared, and (as throughout Ireland) local timber is scarce and of poor quality.

Hemmed in by its countryside, Belfast is a surprisingly rural city. There are still horse-drawn carts; ponies, driven by small boys, rattle through the streets drawing loads of smoking firebrick; a tame goose lives next door to the Ministry of Commerce, not three hundred yards from the City Hall; you may see a blacksmith shoeing horses in Eliza Street, little farther away. There are still many little enclaves of rural housing, like the tiny court at Dunlop's Place off Cromac Street, due (or overdue) for demolition.[2]

Rural in spirit though it be, there is little enough greenery. Its centre is devoid of parks and open spaces; those on the periphery are inadequate, shabby and institutional, despite recent attempts to improve them. Belfast is a grossly overcrowded city—16,836 people live in each square mile, a population density double that of Leeds. Such open spaces as remain are likely to be reminders of the air raids of 1941, when according to the official history of Northern Ireland in the Second World War, in four nights 56,600 houses in Belfast were hit or blasted; indeed, according to the same authority, no other city in the United Kingdom,

---

[1] !

[2] The goose died, and the old Ministry of Commerce was knocked down, in the winter of 1966/7. The blacksmith is gone from Eliza Street; there are very few horse-drawn carts now to be seen; some of the trotting ponies of the redeveloped Markets area are presently housed in cleverly-contrived stabling not a stone's throw from the Royal Courts of Justice. Of the genuine rural survivals, almost all are now gone—the most surprising is still the thatched and whitewashed cottage-farmhouse, perhaps 18th century, with a grove of chestnut trees at its back door, at 41 Sunningdale Park amidst a waste of redbrick suburbia. Less dramatic rivals are Rose Cottage, Coyle's Place, about to be restored by the HEARTH housing association; and Rhubarb Cottage at 36 Ballysillan Road.

save London and possibly Liverpool, lost so many of its citizens in one night's raid. Most of the blitzed ground has been built over again on the old pattern, and the opportunity for planned post-war redevelopment thrown away.

There is mile upon mile of dreary red-brick terrace housing; the population doubled roughly every twenty years throughout the nineteenth century. Mercifully, there are no back-to-backs; but there are slums, and, at last, slum clearance schemes. Despite every discouragement, people take pride in their homes: in the country, the Ulster farmhouse is whitewashed once a year: the tradition has travelled into the city, and thousands of sub-standard houses are painted often and lovingly in gay and cheerful colours.

On the other side of the coin, there is the crystallized history for which Ulster is famous: the crude slogans, the primitive paintings on gable walls of King William III on his white horse crossing the Boyne; the union jacks and tricolours; coarse comments on Paisley or the Pope; the lattice-work arches erected for the twelfth of July, the banners and bonfires and processions. If they were not so tragically in earnest, the politico-religious manifestations of Belfast would rival the Saintes-Maries-de-la-Mer as the last great folk festival of Europe.

Belfast is very much a sea-port. Masts and funnels may be seen at the very foot of High Street; the gantries of the shipyard tower over the south bank of the Lagan. When a large ship is launched, thousands of people—men, women and children—stream into the shipyard to watch, and the whole city takes pride in the achievement of its menfolk. It would be a blow to the heart of Belfast if the shipyard were ever to close.[3]

This book is about the buildings of Belfast, not about its people. But buildings are built by people for people, and it is well never to forget that fact.

This book deals with the period from 1700 to 1914, and with the area of Belfast within its present boundaries; but the city covers twenty-five square miles. I have tried to deal with every building of importance within the central area, and with outstanding or representative buildings in the suburbs and outskirts. I have looked at the outside of every building I mention, and at the inside of some. I set out with the high resolve of going into every church and every public-house in the city; but their numbers defeated me. The Directory shows that there are 265 houses of worship (mostly locked on week-days) and 589 licensed houses (all locked on Sundays).[4] So I may have missed some treasures; but I hope not.

I started in 1700 because I know of no earlier building in the city, save Con O'Neill's Bridge over the Con's Water River, a hoop of ancient stonework crumbling shamefully at the foot of a pylon in the derelict waste-land behind Abetta Parade. I have ended, with reluctance, in 1914. Not because I dislike contemporary architecture as such; though most recent work in Belfast, and especially in the city centre, is banal and mediocre. Were I to speak frankly of the modern buildings of Belfast, I should certainly be sued for defamation by several living architects. But I have a better reason for keeping silence: my inability to discount the influence of passing fashion on my judgements of the work of the past fifty years.

Indeed, fickle fashion all too easily warps and distorts every judgement on architectural

[3]   The gantries have been dismantled, and replaced by the two enormous German-built cranes— Goliath in 1969, and Samson in 1974—which straddle Harland & Wolff's new building dock. Floatings-out, and naming ceremonies, have replaced launches; for security reasons, the public is no longer admitted; but the pride survives.
[4]   The latest edition of the Directory shows 246 houses of worship, and only 245 licensed houses, a startling change. But this narrow election result is overturned if clubs are brought into the reckoning. 182 clubs are shown in the Directory. Of course, not all of these have or want liquor licences; but then again, there are probably still some survivors of the illicit shebeens which sprang up during the worst of the Troubles.

taste. The Victorians and Edwardians came to loathe Georgian architecture, which seemed to them dull, tedious and repetitive. Our immediate predecessors detested and derided the Victorians. Now they are coming back into fashion; but the Edwardian style, and the styles of the inter-war years, are still anathema.[5] I have tried, in all honesty, to educate my eye, and to discriminate between the good and the bad of each period, leaving ephemeral modishness to one side. All judgement is subjective; all human taste is fallible; I shall not quarrel with those who find my opinions unacceptable.

This book represents a venture into wholly unexplored territory. No County History, no local authority list of buildings, no Ancient Monuments Survey, no Pevsner Guide, yet exists for Belfast.[6] An architectural history of Liverpool was published in 1858; another, and an excellent one, in 1964; but no such work, even in note form, has ever to my knowledge been undertaken in Belfast. Accordingly, I have had to bring together a great number of particles of information from a great number of sources, published and unpublished, of varying reliability.

For the years up to 1820, I derived much useful information from the large collection of seventeenth- and eighteenth-century Donegall Estate leases in the Public Record Office of Northern Ireland. For the years after 1859, I have relied largely on the files of that excellent publication, *The Irish Builder*, first published in Dublin under the editorship of J. J. Lyons and still going strong. For the years between 1820 and 1859, I have had to lean heavily on the many maps of Belfast (including the first and admirable Ordnance Survey of 1832) published during this period.

I have employed certain symbols. Asterisks I have used, after the manner of the great   *
Baedeker, to indicate which buildings I think deserve preservation, either on their own merits   **
or as fine examples of a class which must soon disappear. I am not a wholesale preservationist; ***
Belfast greatly needs replanning and redevelopment. An enormous proportion especially of its dwelling-houses are worn out and need replacement.[7] On the other hand, the stout and characteristic merchant palaces of its centre have years of useful life in them. It should not be impossible, in replanning the city, to strike a reasonable balance between renewal and preservation. If we fail to do so, our descendants will certainly reproach us, bitterly and with justification.

I have used the less conventional symbol of crossed swords to indicate that there was a
major quarrel, or scandal, or row, in connection with the design or erection of any building. These were the common change of the architectural profession between 1850 and 1914. We seldom hear of them now, when architects have become as solemn and magisterial as surgeons. Like surgeons, they are very ready to tell us what is wrong with us and what is good for us. I hope my friends in the profession will not mind when I say that architects are overdue for some quiet debunking; they would do well to pay more attention to the views of the consumer, the intelligent layman.[8] I need not say, for I am sure it is painfully evident in the pages that follow, that I have no architectural qualifications whatsoever; but I will fight for my right to criticise the environment that surrounds me.

---

[5] No longer: the best architecture of the Edwardians, and of the inter-war years, is now recognised and admired; the wheel has moved on; it is now the styles of the 1950s and '60s that are anathema.
[6] A very provisional, tentative and inadequate series of listings for Belfast has been promulgated by Historic Monuments and Buildings Branch, Department of the Environment (N.I.); otherwise, this sentence still holds true.
[7] See the introduction to this edition, p. xii.   [8] I see no reason to change or up-date this opinion.

I have departed from the usual practice in works on architecture, and have throughout given the date when a building was completed, rather than the date when it was commenced.

Few citizens seem to have any awareness of their surroundings; the assorted ironmongery that passes for street furniture arouses only a few faint protests; profit seems always to come before amenity; no city can have so many derelict and untended culs-de-sac and corners of waste land. But at long last there is a faint change in the climate of opinion. It is to the credit of the present City Fathers that they have paid some attention in May 1965 to Sir Robert Matthew's Report, published in 1963, on the Belfast Region; and that in May 1965 they appointed planning consultants to advise on the future development of the city. If the publication of this book contributes, in any degree, to a greater awareness of and interest in the appearance of Belfast, it will have served a worth-while purpose.

There are, I am sure, many errors and omissions in this book: I shall welcome corrections. None of the errors are the responsibility of the many people from whom I have received help over the past six years. My particular thanks are due to Mr Kenneth Darwin, Deputy Keeper of the Public Record Office of Northern Ireland, and his staff; to Mr James Vitty, Librarian of the Belfast Linen Hall Library, and his staff; and to the late Mr E. V. Walshe, Planning Officer of Belfast. I owe thanks also to the Director of the National Library of Ireland, Dublin; the Registrar of Deeds, Dublin; the Glasgow City Librarian; the Exeter City Librarian; the Librarian of the Royal Institute of British Architects; and the Curator of Sir John Soane's Museum; all of whom have dealt patiently with my enquiries.

I am especially grateful to the Governors of the Linen Hall Library, Belfast, for their help and support in connection with the publication of this book; and to the Trustees of the Gallaher Mitchell Trust.

Of the illustrations, forty-six were specially taken for this work by Patrick Rossmore, to whom I am deeply indebted, not only for his patience and skill, but also for many enjoyable hours spent at all times of day, and in all weathers, in many corners of Belfast. For permission to reproduce other illustrations (individually noted in the List of Plates) I am grateful to the Trustees of the British Museum; the Trustees of the Ulster Museum; the Director of the National Library of Ireland; the Ministry of Finance for Northern Ireland; the Public Record Office of Northern Ireland; The Queen's University of Belfast; Northern Bank Ltd; Mr E. D. Hill; Dr W. A. McCutcheon; Professor M. J. Boyd; Mr Robert McKinstry; and Mr Leslie Stuart.

Most of all, I am grateful to the very many individuals (far too numerous to name) who showed me round their buildings, told me of their histories, and in many instances went to endless trouble to dredge up records and information about them.

December 1966   C. E. B. Brett

ONE

THE GEORGIAN TOWN

1700—1800

In April, 1706, the third Earl of Donegall, landowner of Belfast and the surrounding countryside, was killed at the siege of Monjuich, fighting in Marlborough's army in the War of the Spanish Succession. Two years later, his unfortunate widow lost three of her six daughters and her home when, on 25 April 1708, Belfast Castle was burned to the ground. It seems to have been a tall semi-fortified Elizabethan manor-house, surrounded by gooseberry-gardens, melon plots, and formal parterres extending as far as a branch of the river Lagan, and up to the ramparts with which Colonel Chichester had fortified the town in 1642 (Plate 4). Whatever the architectural merits of the Castle, its disappearance had lasting consequences for the development of Belfast. First, it deprived the town of its natural focus; since then, Belfast, unlike other fortified towns owing their existence to a strategic site, has lacked a permanent centre of gravity. Second, and more important, it deprived the Chichester family of their home; thenceforward, to the considerable relief of the inhabitants, they became for the most part absentee landlords. Nevertheless, the tastes and habits of the family continued to influence the growth of the town for another century and a half.

Belfast had grown up on the muddy foreshore where the wide and meandering Lagan entered Belfast Lough, at a point where a small tributary, the Farset, flowed into it; this stream flowed down the middle of the High Street and at its foot formed a modest harbour. There were few buildings of any antiquity, perhaps naturally, since the river crossing had many times been a battlefield—Belfast was taken by Edward Bruce in 1315; by The O'Neill in 1476; by the Earl of Kildare thrice between 1503 and 1523; by General Munro in 1644; and by Colonel Monk in 1648. In 1651, the old chapel of the ford, then the parish church of St George, was converted into the Grand Fort and Citadel by Colonel Venables. It was later demilitarized, and still stood until 1774: but apart from the Castle, the church, and a modest Market House, there were few if any houses of more than two storeys; for the most part, Belfast must have consisted of thatched cottages of the cruder sort. A lease of 1670 contains a covenant to build 'one good handsome Englishlike house' of one storey.[1] The town was still very much overshadowed by the nearby harbour of Carrickfergus with its great Norman castle, ancient church, and the stone houses in its Scotch and English Quarters.

From 1706 to 1757 the sole proprietor of Belfast was Arthur Chichester, fourth Earl of Donegall, a childless widower against whom lunacy proceedings were brought by Sir Roger Newdigate (the founder of the Prize for English Verse), which failed by a narrow margin;

---

[1] PRONI: D 509/25: Lease to John Drenon, 1 November 1670.

the fourth Earl was however admitted to be, to say the least, 'rather weak and incapable'. Ultimately, the proceedings were settled in 1754 by the appointment of Thomas Ludford of Warwick, one of the guardians of the infant heir to the title, and another relative, Mr Richard Barry, of Cheshire, as trustees of the estate.

In 1752, Lord Massereene had written to Thomas Ludford: 'I live in the neighbourhood of Belfast and know it to be in a ruinous condition, and will loose both its Trade and Inhabitants if it is not speedily supported by proper Tenures'.[2] Short leases and tenancies, providing no incentive to build or repair, had been the rule; it must be admitted that the leases granted by the fourth Earl under the tutelage of his Trustees were not much better, almost all being for periods of forty-one years.

His nephew, the fifth Earl, was very different; a young man of expensive tastes and extravagant habits, thrice married in later life, and said to enjoy an income of £50,000 a year, he celebrated his uncle's death by buying the Elizabethan manor of Fisherwick, in Staffordshire, in his eighteenth year. As soon as he attained his majority, he called in Capability Brown to rebuild it. The new house was 'a vast Palladian structure' with a great Corinthian portico. Joseph Bonomi was employed as stuccodore; the ceilings were painted by Rigaud. There was a large park, notable for the absence of a ha-ha round the house, in which Brown planted no less than 100,000 trees, mainly oak.[3] Fisherwick did not long survive its owner; Lord Donegall died in 1799; the house was demolished in 1806. He is said to have possessed an immense collection of objects of vertu of great rarity and value, and a splendid library. This was the man upon whose patronage the development of Belfast depended in the second half of the century; and while he confined his more lavish expenditure to the far side of the Irish Sea, he left a considerable mark on the town.

It is very evident that he was viewed with mixed feelings by the townspeople. On the one hand, he was regarded as a harsh absentee, only too ready to evict the surrounding farmers if higher rents could be secured from the Belfast merchants; on the other, his obituary notice in the *Belfast News Letter* of January 1799 was more handsome:

In every part of an extensive landed property it is acknowledged that his Lordship was the kindest and most indulgent Landlord. Though an absentee from this country he evinced his attachment to it by a liberal expenditure of large sums for the advantage of the community. In the course of a few years he laid out above £60,000 in the Lagan Navigation and the Public Buildings in this town.[4]

In 1757, when he succeeded his uncle, Belfast was still a nondescript little town with few buildings of note apart from its *raison d'être*, the Long Bridge across the Lagan. This had been built in 1682 close to the site of an earlier ford, an impressive piece of masonry 2,562 feet long, with twenty-one arches. Unfortunately, in 1692 seven of the arches fell in, having been weakened by the passage of Schomberg's heavy cannon on their way to the Battle of the Boyne. But the bridge was repaired and stood until 1841, when it was replaced by the Queen's Bridge. The lump of stone embedded in the pavement at Mountpottinger cross-roads is said to have formed part of the old Long Bridge. (It is also said, on even less evidence, to· have been King William's mounting-block.)

The fifth Earl adopted a more constructive policy than his predecessor. A careful survey of the whole town was carried out; the old leases were surrendered; and on 20 July 1767, new leases (of which 258 survive in the Public Record Office) were granted for almost every holding in the town. These leases were, in the then current Irish idiom, for the lives of three

2   George Benn, *History of Belfast*, Vol. I (London, 1877), p. 535 n.
3   Dorothy Stroud, *Capability Brown* (London, 1957), pp 92-3.
4   *Belfast News Letter*, 15 January 1799.

named persons, or for ninety-nine years, whichever might be the longer. Many of them contain beautifully detailed ground plans. It is possible, for example, to identify the rope-walk and potato gardens outside the Ramparts which now comprise the yard of Torrens' Market off Garfield Street; and to trace the brew-houses, cow-houses and stables belonging to the houses lying between Castle Place and Rosemary Street. Most important of all, the great majority of these simultaneous leases imposed obligations on the lessees to build; and to build to a higher standard than had previously been known.

A fair sample is the lease [5] of a house, cowhouse, and yards in Castle Street (roughly where the Ulster Club now stands [6]) to Elizabeth Byrtt, widow. In exchange for her lease, she was required to covenant within fourteen years to take down the building then on the site; and in the stead thereof, 'in a good and workmanlike Manner, and with good sound Materials, to erect, build and finish . . . one good and substantial Messuage or Tenement of Brick and Lime, or Stone and Lime . . . the front . . . to be sashed, and the Roof thereof to be well slated, and all the Side-Walls . . . to be built Twenty-eight Feet high . . . and fourteen Inches thick at least, and that all the Girders, Joists and Roofing, and other Timbers, . . . shall be of good Oak or Fir, and of proper Scantlings respectively: and also shall . . . cause all the Ground . . . to the Middle of the Street . . . to be well paved with Stones or Pebbles.' Sensibly if humiliatingly, the Lease provided also that if 'Elizabeth Byrtt . . . or any person dwelling or residing on . . . the demised premises, or any person by their or any of their order . . . should lay or put upon any part of the Streets of the said town of Belfast, any Ashes, Dung, Filth, or Dirt whatsoever, and suffer the same to lie or continue there above the Space of twenty-four hours,' she should pay 'one shilling for every Parcel of such Ashes, Dung, Filth or Dirt for every day the same should lie.'

Lesser citizens covenanted for houses of lesser size; the scale descended from twenty-eight feet high in Castle Place, to twenty-five in High Street, to eighteen feet in Ann Street, to fifteen feet in Church Lane, to 'cabbins' ten feet high in Carrickfergus Peter's Hill. Not that these heights were necessarily uniform within the same street; but in general, a suitable standard prevailed.

Merchants, on the other hand, were expected to make even more substantial contributions to reconstruction; Thomas Greg was required not only to build two or more good and substantial houses facing the Common Town Dock, but also a good and substantial quay wall of stone and lime 320 feet long, filled and paved to a depth of thirty-five feet; and a draw-bridge across the east end of the dock of sufficient strength to carry loaded carts and carriages, and to constitute (once built) a public right of way.[7]

Only a handful of houses of this period survive unmutilated. At 52-60 Great Patrick Street [8] (c. 1770) are four tiny two-storey cottagey little houses, with hinged casement **
windows upstairs, set far out in front of the building line of the street—first laid out before 1767, but mainly the line of the 1804-09 development (Plate 6). There must have been hundreds of small houses like these surrounding central Belfast at this period.

Still more surprising survivals are 1-5 Pottinger's Court,[9] off Pottinger's Entry, a few **
yards from High Street: three-storey brick houses of the same date, with unrecessed windows (some in pairs), and wooden shutters on the ground floor, still used as private houses.

---

5 PRONI: D 509/191: Lease to Elizabeth Byrtt, 20 July 1767.
6 Alas, no longer: See note 49 on page 37.
7 PRONI: D 509/227: Lease to Thomas Greg, 20 July 1767.
8 Demolished for the Dunbar Street Link Road.
9 Demolished, and the site redeveloped.

The earliest public building now surviving was built in 1769, as a modest single-storey arcaded market-house, by an unknown architect, near the centre of the town at the 'Four Corners'. Seven years later, Lord Donegall at his own expense added an upper floor, containing 'very spacious and elegant' Assembly Rooms (Plate 3). For these, a really first-class London architect was called in: Robert Taylor, one of the last and greatest of the English Palladians, then at the height of his fame, having recently succeeded Sir William Chambers as Architect of the King's Works, and shortly to be knighted. It is not clear whether the exterior (of stone from Dunmurry, near Belfast) was built to Taylor's designs; this seems unlikely, as it was in the highest degree unassuming; the building was completed under the supervision of a Mr Cooper, who seems to have been one of Taylor's assistants. The interior, illustrated in aquatint by Thomas Malton, was very splendid for a provincial market town, with a vaulted and coffered ceiling, Corinthian pilasters, and ornamental plasterwork foreshadowing the designs of the Adam brothers. An estimate for the carved work by a local craftsman, James Forbes, still survives. He was prepared to execute 'Corinthian Pilaster Capitals, 13 inches diameter, at One Guinea and a Half each—Deal mouldings, great and small, viz. Ovolos, Hollows, Ogees, Beads and Fascias, at 6d per foot. Mahogany mouldings at 9d per foot. Guiloches at one shilling per foot—Frizes over doors at Two guineas each—Pateras, eight shillings each.' The work, however, was entrusted to an English carver, one Samuel Kirke. But on his arrival, Kirke engaged both Forbes and Forbes' boy as assistants, and proceeded to leave the work to them while he drank himself to death: on 1 September 1773, Lord Donegall's agent wrote: 'I have . . . to acquaint you of the death of Kirke the carver who I believe brought on a Jaundice and Dropsy by Dram-Drinking—There has been so little work done lately by him at the Exchange that the carpenters are nearly set idle—I believe Forbes who has wrought there could finish the work in as masterly a manner as he could have done'.[10] Unhappily this building, though still standing and now the head office of the Belfast Bank, is totally invisible, having been Victorianized inside and out. For its subsequent fate, see page 30.

***   Lord Donegall's contribution to the Poorhouse, now Clifton House, in North Queen Street, was more modest; he presented the site, but the rest of the cost was borne by public subscription. Opened in 1774, it has generally been attributed to Thomas Cooley of Dublin, who certainly was consulted by the building committee; as also was the Scottish architect Robert Mylne,[11] who prepared sketches for it. But Dr R. W. M. Strain, the historian and present physician of the Belfast Charitable Society, has shown that in fact the amateur plans of Robert Joy, a Belfast paper merchant, were probably those ultimately adopted.[12] The pedimented brick façade, with its stone spire, remains quite unaltered, a very pleasing example of modest Irish Georgian public building, recently renovated and repainted most sympathetically (Plate 2). As well as the poorhouse and the infirmary, the building contained a large room where Assemblies and Balls were held to raise funds for the establishment.

Probably the eventual design was the outcome of many *ad hoc* decisions by committee and craftsmen. One Edward Foot, who also worked under Cooper on the Exchange and seems to have been Lord Donegall's jobbing builder, was appointed superintendent of works in July 1771, but was soon sacked. No successor was appointed. The masons were Joseph McNary for the East wing and William Anderson for the West, with Peter McMeekin and

[10] Donegall Estate Letter-Book, June 1771—January 1774, in possession of John D. Stewart, Belfast (copy in PRONI, ref. T 1893).
[11] A. E. Richardson, *Robert Mylne* (London, 1955), pp 43, 86.
[12] R. W. M. Strain, *Belfast and its Charitable Society* (Oxford, 1961), p. 35.

James Brown. Hugh Dunlap—a considerable speculative builder in his own right—was master carpenter, and modelled a cupola for the committee to consider, and reject, as an alternative to the spire. The coppersmith was a Mr Watson.

The wings were extended in 1821 and 1825. The Charters wing was added in 1868, to the designs of W. J. Barre, author of the polar bears' picnic at Banbridge (the Crozier memorial; see page 39); the Benn wing in 1872 by William Hastings; and the dining hall in 1887, by Godfrey W. Ferguson. By a happy chance, none of the additions are incongruous; the Poorhouse, with its slightly sooty garden, remains a comparatively large island of charm amidst an ocean of chimneys; and still fulfils something very close to its original function.

The new parish church of St Anne (completed 1776; demolished 1900 to make way for St Anne's Cathedral) was built at the sole expense of Lord Donegall (Plate 12). Making use, no doubt, of his Staffordshire contacts, he secured designs from the Warwickshire architect Francis Hiorne (known to Lord Donegall's agent as 'Mr Irons of Warwick'),[13] a specialist in gingerbread-Gothick church design.[14] Of Hiorne's church at Tetbury, Gloucestershire, begun in 1777, Sir Kenneth Clark says that it was a very slim, elegant, insecure eighteenth-century translation of a Gothic church, built like a theatre. 'We feel that Tetbury would collapse at a push'.[15] St Anne's, though not a Gothic building, also proved somewhat insecure; the steeple proved too unsafe to hang the bell; and the original portico had to be taken down and rebuilt. It was described as 'consisting of a nave and chancel, with a lofty Ionic tower surmounted by a Corinthian cupola covered with copper, forming an interesting and conspicuous object for many miles around'.[16]

One of those who assisted Hiorne in the building of St Anne's was Roger Mulholland (1740-1818), a somewhat enigmatic figure about whom all too little is known;[17] but clearly the dominating architect of late eighteenth-century Belfast. He was very active between 1781 and 1799, and during that period undertook much work for Lord Donegall, and took many leases of ground for speculative ventures of his own. In the first lease made to him in 1783 he was described as 'carpenter'; by 1786, when he took a lease of eight acres in Cromack Wood, he had become 'architect'. Whatever his beginnings, he seems to have been a man of some culture. His name appears in the list of 225 original subscribers in 1780 to Pool & Cash's *Views of Dublin*; in 1778 he was one of the founder members of the Belfast Reading Society (now the Linen Hall Library), to which he presented the three volumes of the *Vitruvius Britannicus* and Caesar's *Commentaries* (translated by Duncan).[18] He was also a founder member of that highly political and idealistic body, the Belfast 1st Volunteer Company; but in 1781 was stigmatized as 'a Very Bad Attender'.[19]

By far his most distinguished work was the First Presbyterian (now Unitarian) Church   ***
in Rosemary Street, a delightful building completed in 1783 (Plates 8 and 9).[20] The elliptical interior, with its radial plastered ceiling and beautiful woodwork, remains charming

[13]   Donegall Estate Letter-Book, December 1773; see note 10.
[14]   *Historic Memorials of the First Presbyterian Church* (Belfast, 1887), p. 21.
[15]   Kenneth Clark, *The Gothic Revival* (London, 3rd Ed., 1962), p. 35.
[16]   Samuel Lewis, *Topographical Dictionary of Ireland*, Vol. I (London, 1837), p. 197.
[17]   But see *Roger Mulholland, Architect, of Belfast* (Belfast, 1976), by the present author.
[18]   John Anderson, *History of Linen Hall Library* (Belfast, 1888) p. 22.
[19]   George Benn, *op. cit.*, Vol. I, p. 754.
[20]   Extensively damaged by five large bombs in the vicinity between 1972 and 1975, but happily very well restored, with a completely new ceiling more nearly approaching the original design. Interior repainted in green and white; the touches of gilding, in the ceiling rosettes and the capitals of the columns bearing the gallery, perhaps a bit fussy. See also Tom Moore, *History of First Presbyterian Church, Belfast* (Belfast, 1983).

despite the extension of the east end in the mid-nineteenth-century to allow for an organ behind the pulpit. The classical exterior was unhappily ruined by coarse reconstruction in 1833. But inside, the whole church is an enchanting boat-like composition of curves; on the floor, the oval pattern of box-pews; above, the gallery, borne on wooden Corinthian columns, with the elegant double bow-front of a sideboard, ornamented with wreaths and urns. There are excellent regency and classical memorial tablets on the walls; and a pleasing pulpit with a curving staircase. The sounding-board of the pulpit was removed in 1862 (it is now used as a vestry table), and was found to bear the inscription: 'This meeti...g-house was erected by the inhabitants of Belfast under the care and inspection of Mr Roger Mulholland, who executed the same, both external and internal parts thereof, 1783—this piece executed by Patrick Smyth'. According to the *Historic Memorials* of the congregation, Francis Hiorne took a great interest in the structure, and furnished valuable suggestions, especially as regards the pewing of the interior.

Unhappily most of the woodwork has recently been stripped of its patina and repolished in an attempt to restore the interior to its original appearance. It may be seen at its best during the annual carol service, when hundreds of candles accentuate the elegance of the curves, and their light softens the hardness of too-new-redecoration.

John Wesley, who preached there in 1789, wrote in his journal: 'It is the completest place of worship I have ever seen. It is of oval form; as I judge by my eye a hundred feet long, and seventy or eighty feet broad. It is very lofty, and has two rows of large windows, so that it is as light as our new chapel in London. And the rows of pillars, with every other part, are so finely proportioned, that it is beautiful in the highest degree'; all this despite the fact that he was refused permission to preach there a second time on account of the thieving of the congregation during his sermon.[21] The Earl of Bristol and Bishop of Derry, that redoubtable gourmet of architecture, builder of Ballyscullion, Downhill and Ickworth, declared that 'the beauty of the building does equal honour to the taste of the subscribers and the talent of the architect'; and capped the compliment with a subscription of fifty guineas.

The Second Presbyterian Congregation built a church just behind the first in 1790 (architect unknown; demolished, infamously, to make way for a private car park in 1964). This building had an excellent classical façade, stucco on stone, and a balcony on two sides supported by Roman Ionic oak columns. It is said to have had remarkable acoustics; but in recent years had been used as a furniture factory, and sawing drowned the parson's cough. Though derelict, the front was not much mutilated; it could and should have been preserved.

In the course of the 1780s and '90s, Lord Donegall undertook a number of substantial town-planning schemes. The first and most extensive of these was the development of Donegall Street, Church Street, Talbot Street and Academy Street around St Anne's. This development was entrusted exclusively to Roger Mulholland, who took building leases and covenanted to build substantial and uniform houses within specified periods. A number of these buildings survive, though all have been much mutilated and are now used as shops and offices: 69 Donegall Street [22] (1789) was built as the Vicarage, originally a large and dignified brick house, now shopped, stuccoed, and barely recognizable; 2-8 Talbot Street,[23] (1795) and 56-8 Donegall Street (1793) are other survivors.

---

21 George Benn, *op. cit.*, Vol. I, p. 422.
22 Bomb-damaged, and demolished to provide car-parking space around the cathedral.
23 Demolished.

The rebuilding was later extended up Donegall Street to the Poorhouse; 1 North Queen Street and 207-15 Donegall Street [24] were built in 1792 by one James Cooper, publican, who covenanted to build them 'the cornices doors and windows to range in line with the houses nearest the church of Belfast standing in the same street or so nearly thereto as the run of the ground will permit without inconvenience or injury'.[25] This is now the wreckage of a fine terrace; its neighbours 201-5 Donegall Street [26]—built in 1799 by John Milford, linen-draper—are a little smaller and later, but rather less spoiled.

Another major venture was the building in 1785 of the White Linen Hall (where the City Hall now stands), and the laying out of Linen Hall Street (now Donegall Place) as the upper-class residential area of the town. It was the linen, not the Linen Hall, that was white; a market for unbleached linen (the Brown Linen Hall) had been opened in 1754 in Donegall Street, and rebuilt in 1773 on another site in the same street. Although the venture was under the patronage of Lord Donegall, who contributed the ground, the funds in the main came from private subscriptions: no less than £17,550 was raised, including £100 from Roger Mulholland (who was probably the architect of the building, though this is not certain), and, incidentally, £100 from Charles Brett. The White Linen Hall, demolished in 1898, was a rather plain two-storeyed stone building built round a large open quadrangle; apart from heavy quoins, round-headed windows in the central block, and Venetian windows at the terminal blocks, it was almost bare of ornament; it was felt to be too plain, and a cupola was added in 1815 (Plate 11). For almost a century it accommodated the books and reading-room of the Linen Hall Library, as well as performing more commercial functions.

The large and impressive terrace houses built by Roger Mulholland in Donegall Place were likewise much less ornamental than would have been their contemporary equivalents in Dublin; it seems clear that none of them displayed the elegant fanlights, porticoes or plasterwork then in fashion in the capital. But they were substantial nonetheless, and commanded high rents. One of them was leased in 1791 to the Rev. Edward Patterson, at a rent of £34 2s 6d; he was, however, allowed an abatement in the last year's rent of £11 16s 0d, being half the cost of all the locks, grates, chimney pieces, and shelves in the building;[27] another was occupied by the redoubtable and philanthropic Dr James McDonnell, of the Glens, ultimately the last private resident in what became the shopping centre of the city. Only 27 Donegall Place survives of the original street in recognizable form; and it has been stuccoed and classicized in the Victorian manner.

The third planning scheme of these years, though a very much lesser one, was the development of Smithfield, laid out in July 1788 around the old corn and hide market known as 'the Rails'. 69 Smithfield [28] is probably a relic of this scheme, and, if so, was built by Miss Olivia Tombs.

A number of less substantial eighteenth-century buildings are still standing, most of them altered very largely from their original state. There are at any rate two pubs. Kelly's Cellars, 30-2 Bank Street, built about 1780, has a pleasant whitewashed outside; the downstairs rooms, with knee-height bar, low archways, and blackened snugs, are highly interesting and

---

[24] Still standing, but only just: all blocked up except two ground-floor shops; due for demolition to make way for—a traffic roundabout.
[25] PRONI: D 509/783: Lease to James Cooper, 6 June 1790.
[26] Likewise all blocked up, and destined to become the roundabout.
[27] PRONI: Lease to Rev. Edward Patterson, 2 May 1791.
[28] Demolished after repeated bombs.

atmospheric if now somewhat self-conscious;[29] the upstairs bar is, however, aesthetically deplorable. If local legend is to be believed, the United Irishmen when plotting divided their time between these cellars and a secret room in the roof-space of the second Presbyterian Church in Rosemary Street; true or not, this nicely symbolizes the alliance upon which their plots were founded.

White's Tavern, 1-9 Winecellar Entry, was rebuilt in 1790 as a spirit warehouse by the Valentine Jones, wine merchant, who, at the age of ninety, danced a celebrated contre-danse in the Assembly Rooms with his son, grandson, and great-grandson, all Valentine Joneses. Until quite recently, it combined the picturesque and the practical to perfection, with its heavy timbered bays, barred windows and roof hoist. Unfortunately it has recently been disastrously restored in the 'Ye Olde' style; the outside boasts a poker-work inn-sign, the interior is replete with arty brass and electric bulbs in bogus lanterns.

Du Barry's pub, 6 Prince's Street,[30] a haunt of sailors nowadays, boasts more-than-eighteenth-century-bottle-bottomed panes between the glazing bars amidst the pebble-dash.

College Court, a pokey alley running from Castle Street to College Street, conceals a mysteriously un-numbered large whitewashed Georgian dwelling-house of the better sort, with a nice (though later) porch, and tubbed trees; this seems to be where the policemen of Queen Street house their families.

Torrens' Market is an attractive large colour-washed house in a large yard at 21 Garfield Street, with a rural outside staircase in the Scottish manner; presumably built by some member of the Simms family whose tanyard, ropewalk and garden occupied the site from 1767 to 1825.

No visible part now remains of the first Roman Catholic church in Belfast, St Mary's, Chapel Lane, opened on 30 May 1784. The ceremonies were remarkable in the history of Belfast for the warmly ecumenical spirit displayed by the Protestant inhabitants, a spirit which alas was dissipated over the next fifty years and has never returned. The 1st Belfast Volunteer Company, under command of Captain Waddell Cunningham, lined the chapel yard as a guard of honour, in full dress, and presented arms to the priest as he passed into the church to celebrate Mass; substantial contributions to the cost of the building were received from the Protestant inhabitants.[31] This, however, was at the opening of that brief golden age in Belfast when the spirit of the United Irishmen, and later the liberal ideals of the French Revolution, fired the imagination of the inhabitants. Indeed, Bastille Day was celebrated in 1791 with a review of six thousand Volunteers, a great procession through the streets, and a feast in the White Linen Hall.

One Catholic memorial of earlier and unhappier days remains; Friar's Bush graveyard, Stranmillis Road, is the place where during the penal days open-air Mass was celebrated on an oak table in a sand-pit. The caretaker's cottage at the entrance is now empty, the gates locked, many of the older graves submerged in nettles and mare's tail;[32] the crumbling

---

[29]   Now not quite so atmospheric as it used to be, after a half-hearted 'renovation'; but still worth a visit. Astoundingly, the present front exterior turns out to have been designed in the late 1940's or early '50s by the late Henry Lynch Robinson, and the curly lamp-bracket by Max Clendinning: (information from Mr Robert McKinstry).

[30]   Still surviving, just; its romantic (or sleazy) associations would well justify a sensitive rehabilitation.

[31]   James O'Laverty, *History of Diocese of Down and Connor*, Vol. II (Dublin, 1880), p. 409.

[32]   Now greatly tidied up, and put into pretty good order, mostly by volunteers; though some of the tombs have been smashed, the cottage seems to be empty again, and the gates are still usually locked.

monuments against the walls are overlooked on one side by the tall ugly mass of the Ulster Museum, on another by the still taller and uglier mass of the University's Keir Building; it remains nevertheless a soothing resort for melancholy, in the blessed absence of tarmacadam, granite chippings and white marble.

The equally evocative, but better tended,[33] graveyard behind the Poorhouse was opened in 1798. The much older Shankill graveyard is now a rather bare municipal garden.

One or two other eighteenth-century remnants deserve a brief mention. Robb's department store, 1-15 Castle Place,[34] still includes in its façade the original pilastered front and architraved windows erected by Thomas Sheridan in 1786 when he rebuilt the Donegall Arms Hotel.

24 Arthur Street has a pleasing fanlight on its Arthur Place side; this was no doubt the front door to the house of James Hunter, architect, who lived here in 1802; the building being probably ten years earlier. 26 Arthur Street,[35] though Victorian stucco to the street, has attractive twin round staircases with unrecessed windows at the back, and seems to date from the 1780s, at which time the staircase windows can have overlooked little but slob and the shallow waters of the Lagan.

Other buildings probably of this period include: 16 Commercial Court;[36] 21 Exchange Street West,[37] a strange two-storey little house, with a corner doorway and wide windows under broad timber lintels; 20-2 Edward Street,[38] with an unusual under-the-eaves attic storey and unrecessed windows; 4-14 Church Lane;[39] 14 Waring Street;[40] and 32-50 Princes Street.[41] There are also a number of eighteenth-century houses in Millfield (now ripe for demolition and clearance), including the squalid but attractive old inn, 85 Millfield, on the corner of Brown Street, and 6 Brown Street next door—very likely 56-8 and 66-8 Brown Street also—all these developed by the original Belfast Capitalist, John Brown, linen draper and Sovereign of the town from 1797 to 1801, as also the curious curved corner shop where Brown Street meets Sackville Street.[42]

There were no great mansions in the immediately surrounding countryside. Perhaps mention should be made of the parish church at Newtownbreda, however, a small village then some four miles from the town but now just outside the city boundary: built in 1747,[43] for the Dowager Viscountess Middleton, reputedly to the plans of the German-born Dublin practitioner Richard Cassels (author of Carton, Co. Kildare, Powerscourt, Co. Wicklow, and Westport House, Co. Mayo), it is modest and rural externally; the interior is pleasing but not greatly distinguished. The chancel, decorated with pairs of Ionic pilasters, was added in 1883 to plans by Sir Thomas Drew, but is entirely in keeping with the original church; there are embryonic semicircular transepts, and a rather plain gallery (also added in 1883, and also quite in keeping) squeezed uncomfortably close to the vaulted ceiling. The churchyard contains some good monuments, in particular the mausoleum of Thomas Greg (died 1796), with coupled Doric columns at the corners, urns, and festoons.

---

[33] No longer true, alas: despite great efforts to tidy it, the Clifton Street graveyard has been shockingly vandalised, and is now in a lamentable condition. See Introduction, page xiv.

[34] Severely bomb-damaged, but very crudely patched up: only the capital of one single pilaster survived (not the bomb but) the repairs.

[35] 24 and 26 Arthur Street were both, unhappily, knocked down to make way for Cawood's 'box' office. James Hunter's fanlight was rescued and is in the care of the author, awaiting a new home.

[36] Bombed.

[37] 21 Exchange Street West should have read '1 Edward Street': demolished all the same.

[38] 20-2 Edward Street are, surprisingly, still there—they and a few modest neighbours well worth saving.

[39] 4-14 Church Lane: surviving with fortitude, despite many nearby bombs and the shadow of the impending multi-storey car park.

[40] Bombed.   [41] Demolished.

[42] All the houses mentioned in Millfield, Brown Street, and Sackville Street, have now been swept away by redevelopment.

[43] Or perhaps earlier: the *Archaeological Survey of County Down* (Belfast, 1966), p. 333, says "c. 1737" but without citing any authority.

TWO

LATE GEORGIAN BELFAST

1800—1837

In 1799, the fifth Earl of Donegall (who had been promoted in 1791 to the rank of Marquis) died, and was succeeded by his eldest son, George Augustus, then aged thirty. There is a curious absence of information [1] about this young man, and a reticence on the part of local historians. It is clear, however, that he ran up staggering debts; in 1847, three years after his death, the estate was incumbered to the tune of no less than £408,000,[2] and ultimately, as will be seen, the leasehold reversions throughout Belfast were sold through the Incumbered Estates Court to the inhabitants, to the lasting benefit of the latter.

Just when the process started, or on what extravagances the money was squandered, it seems now impossible to ascertain. George Benn, the charitably disposed historian of Belfast, in the second volume of his work (published in 1880) quoted from an unnamed source: 'Immediately after the 5th January, 1799, the houses in Duke's Place, and other favourite dwelling-places of the children of Israel, were brilliantly illuminated. Rum and cakes were distributed in abundance; and the children of the circumcised rejoiced exceedingly, not because the deceased peer had acquired an evil reputation as a persecutor of the people, for indeed he had never been known to have any dealings with the tribe, but because on his death many of the Jews came into large possessions.' Benn says that the account of the outward demonstrations is untrue; but adds, enigmatically, 'the meaning conveyed by this will be easily comprehended by the people of Belfast'.[3] Probably his downfall was gambling; in 1802, that agreeable rattle Mrs McTier wrote to Dr Drennan in Dublin, 'Lord Donegall was in treaty with (Viscount) Dungannon for Belvoir, but out of £2,000 a year, said to be his present reduction from last year's £10,000, he cannot give £1,500 for a house—he therefore goes in to Tom Stewart's . . . then I suppose will be the consummation of gambling, vanity and ruin of our society'.[4]

Another ray of light is thrown on the subject when Benn records that in January 1808, a great complimentary entertainment was given to the Marquis by two hundred of his tenantry; that the Marquis was lauded as the best and kindest and most liberal landlord in

---

[1] No longer; W. A. Maguire has illuminated the sorry career of this nobleman in *Living like a Lord* (Belfast, 1984), and elsewhere.
[2] PRONI: T 956/140: Petition of John Turner, 1849.
[3] George Benn, *op. cit.*, Vol II, p. 10.
[4] PRONI: Drennan Letters: Mrs McTier to Dr Drennan, 8 March 1802.

all Ireland; and that there were illuminations and rejoicings at the same time at Doagh and Fisherwick: 'but no intimation is given of the cause. Could it have been on account of a great defeat the Jew brokers of London sustained a few months before from the Marquis in Chancery in Dublin?' [5]

As to his character, Benn merely remarks, 'it was soon discovered that the second Marquis did not possess the abilities of his father; that while kind, benevolent, and always generous to the town, he was destitute of that firmness of character, and that commanding talent, necessary to deal with so great and rising a place as Belfast.' Unlike his father, he was not an absentee; he lived in modest discomfort at first in Donegall Square, in a house to which he could not afford to get up a doorcase,[6] and later at Ormeau,[7] an inconvenient house in a Tudorish style on the outskirts of the town; and used to walk in the streets, or ride through them on a little pony, in the most unostentatious manner—a marked contrast to the flamboyance of his father.

The age of patronage had ended for Belfast; the citizens were thrown back on their resources where expenditure for the public welfare was concerned. As Mrs McTier shrewdly remarked in a letter on 21 November 1803, 'Belfast is really improving very fast, and though the landlord cannot do much for it at *his own* expense, yet want of money may operate to its advantage.' [8] Indeed, in view of the liberal and enlightened opinions common amongst the inhabitants of Belfast in the last two decades of the eighteenth century, much might have been expected of them. But at the opening of the century there was much to depress the progressive-minded. The rising of the United Irishmen in 1798 had been quelled, and their Belfast leader, Henry Joy McCracken, publicly hanged outside the Market House. In 1800, the Act of Union with England had been forced through the Irish Parliament by a combination of cajolery and corruption. Catholic emancipation had suffered a setback, and was not to be attained until 1829. The Napoleonic Wars dragged on and on; in Ireland, as in England, the wartime patriotism of the establishment bore harshly on those holding unconventional or suspect views. In addition, the continental blockade caused much economic hardship; the textile trade was at a standstill for want of access to its markets; the building trade was often at a standstill for want of materials.

During the first ten years or so of the century, indeed, building leases continued to be granted and the town continued to expand. But more and more the covenants were not complied with and the ground had to be leased out a second time. An ambitious scheme for laying out a Great George's Square near the harbour, on the Edinburgh model, was started in 1804,[9] but soon abandoned. North Parade and South Parade—now Chichester Street and Wellington Place respectively—which had been commenced as superior terraces at right angles to Donegall Place in the 1790s, proceeded slowly, but neither scheme was completed.

Some fine buildings of this period, however, still stand; and the quality of their construction is surprisingly high considering the severe shortages of materials (especially sound timber) at this time.

The *Belfast Monthly Magazine* repeatedly commented on these shortages; for example, in February 1808: 'Much distress must necessarily result to the different classes of workmen

---

5   George Benn, *op. cit.*, Vol II, p.63.
6   PRONI: Drennan Letters: Mrs McTier to Dr Drennan, 11 March 1805.
7   See now W. A. Maguire, 'The Second Marquis of Donegall at Ormeau', in *Proceedings of R.I.A.*, Vol. 83, C, No. 15, 1983.
8   PRONI: Drennan Letters: Mrs McTier to Dr Drennan, 21 November 1803.
9   PRONI: D 509/1543: Lease to T. L. Stewart, 1 October 1804.

Belfast is very much a
seaport; the Clarendon No. 1
Graving Dock, started in
1796 and finished in 1800, is
now disused, but still intact.

2

Pl. 2: The Poorhouse, now Clifton House, finished in 1774, is still externally quite unaltered. Pl. 3: The new Market House and Assembly Rooms were completed to plans by Sir Robert Taylor in 1775; then Head Office of the Belfast Bank; now a branch of the Northern Bank. Pl. 4: Thomas Phillips, a fortification engineer, mapped Belfast in 1685. The old Castle was burned in 1708; the Market House demolished in 1802.

3

4

5

6

Grand people lived in grand houses; lesser folk in tiny ones. Pl. 5: Nos. 7 and 9
Chichester Street were built as dwellings in 1804: twice bombed but repaired. Pl. 6: Nos.
52-60 Great Patrick Street date from about 1770: demolished for road works. Pl. 7: The
top of Donegall Street about 1815, showing the Poorhouse, and St Patrick's Chapel,
pinnacles and all: the terraces in between now blocked up, due for demolition for a traffic
roundabout.

7

8

Pls. 8 and 9: The charming elliptical
church in Rosemary Street was built by
Roger Mulholland in 1783. Its exterior was
altered and spoiled in 1833; bomb-damaged
but restored. Behind it, on the left, stood
the second Presbyterian church, completed
in 1790, and demolished (to make room for
a private car park) in 1964.

9

Pl. 10: The body of St George's church, High Street, was completed in 1816 by the Dublin architect John Bowden; but the portico, probably designed by Michael Shanaghan, originally formed part of the curved facade of Ballyscullion House, built by the Earl-Bishop of Derry in 1788. Bomb damage to the church itself repaired, but not so its surroundings.

11

Three cupolas, all long since disappeared:
Pl. 11: The White Linen Hall was built in
1785; the cupola added only in 1815. That
of St Anne's church (Pl. 12) was built to
plans by Francis Hiorne of Warwick in
1776. Pl. 13: Francis Johnston's drawing for
the Lunatic Asylum built in 1829 on the
Falls Road.

12

13

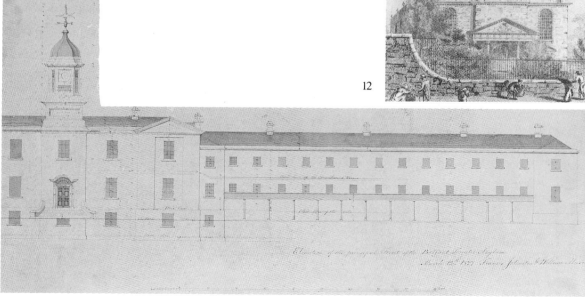

Pl. 14: The Academical Institution, finished in 1814, is a greatly simplified version of Sir John Soane's original concept. Pl. 15: The very handsome Commercial Buildings were erected in 1822 under the supervision of one John McCutcheon; the plans were clearly from a more sophisticated hand. Tha statuary figures, alas, were never executed.

15

Naïve Gothical and naïve Classical both flourished in the years before Victoria's accession. Pl. 16: Detail of a charming terrace in Donegall Pass (notice the roundel door): bombed, vandalised and demolished. Pl. 17: The dignified vernacular gateway to the Durham Street Mill: bombed and demolished.

16

17

employed in the several branches of building, from the present exorbitant prices of timber'; and in August of the same year, 'Timber continues enormously high; one vessel, we believe the first and only one, has arrived at Belfast from Norway under neutral colours, but the small supply had little effect on the market . . . Vessels are going out to Nova Scotia, and other parts of British America, with workmen from these countries to cut down timber from their immense forests.'

On the other hand, the appearance of the town a few years later seems to have been spoiled by a superfluity of visible timber; in a work called *The Irish Builder's Guide*, published in 1813 by Thomas Humphreys, Measurer, and dedicated to Francis Johnston, the author writes: 'I will beg to arrest the attention of the gentlemen and merchants of Belfast, while I observe to them, that their taste in architecture needs a little refinement, particularly, they ought to endeavour to remove that odious appearance which almost all their new buildings, of whatever denomination, have, by being for years after they are built, propped by large beams at every angle, until the lime and brick gets sufficient time to cement. Having spent some time in Belfast, I endeavoured to discover the cause of this tottering appearance: . . . an overrated economy in the employer, and no deficiency in the workman.'

7-11 Chichester Street [10] were built, as part of a larger terrace, in 1804.[11] 11 has been *** shopped; but 7 and 9 are almost entirely unspoilt four-storey-and-basement tall brick terrace houses, with high steps up to Doric-columned sandstone doorcases (Plate 5). 9 has lost its fanlight; 7 has had plaster window reveals added to match 9, which was probably the central house of the original terrace. Both have their glazing-bars complete.

4 Donegall Square South [12] is the sole survivor of a terrace of nine more sophisticated *** large houses built about 1808 by Adam McClean,[13] a draper, one of the four fortune-seeking sons of the innkeeper at Shane's Castle, Co. Antrim. That he was genuinely interested in architecture and not merely in property speculation may be deduced from the tedious and rather pathetic letters, still preserved, with which in later years he bombarded the great Sir John Soane.[14] The ground floor is of rusticated stone, and has round-headed windows; the cornice is ornamented; the standard of the ironwork is high. His architect is unknown; both this and the previous terrace could well be the work of Roger Mulholland who was still active in Belfast; but there is no evidence that this is so.

It is worth noticing the fearful fate that in 1960 overtook the similar house next door, No. 5, when it was mercilessly 'restored': a new front wall was built with arty little bricks; key stones were inserted, but the dentils below the cornice were omitted; coy tear-drop glazing bars were installed and flanked with shutters; and a spurious fanlight, balcony and railings were added. It would be hard to find a better architectural example of the honest woman flanked by her fallen sister.

84 and 86 Donegall Street,[15] built about 1809, still retain their original arched doorways with fluted Ionic columns; 86 is cheerfully painted. On a different level, it is worth noting that the terrace of small two-storey cottage-type stuccoed houses at 24-38 Gordon Street,[16] due very soon for demolition, can be dated with some accuracy to the year 1802.[17]

---

10   All three twice seriously damaged by car-bombs in the alley at the rear; the former returns and stables completely destroyed, the front parts restored. A very successful new shop-front inserted in No. 11.

11   Registry of Deeds, Dublin: Lease of 1 June 1803.   12   Bombed and demolished.
13   Lease to A. McClean, 5 January 1805.   14   Sir John Soane's Museum, London.
15   Demolished.   16   Demolished.
17   PRONI: D 509/1366: Lease to John Taylor, 5 June 1802.

Although private building remained at a low ebb, a series of public buildings was erected at the public expense in the second decade of the new century. The first of these was the Lancasterian School built in Frederick Street in 1811, to provide education on the economical principles enunciated by Joseph Lancaster: the teacher taught the eldest children; they passed on what they had learned to the next eldest; and so downwards. Demolished in 1963, this was an austere and dignified symmetrical two-storeyed building, originally brick but later stuccoed, with a hipped roof, a formal but discreet stone Doric porch, and plain pilasters. Incredibly its builders were attacked by critics in the correspondence columns of the *Belfast Monthly Magazine* for 'ostentatious display of architecture': yet its merit, which was considerable, lay entirely in its good proportions, the long bulk broken only by the pattern of doorways and glazing-barred windows; indeed the stone cornice and quoins were omitted from the rear in the interests of economy. Plain as it was, it cost £1,954 7s 10½d to build; in the first year, over twelve thousand boys and girls received daily or Sunday schooling there.[18]

A year later, a similar but slightly smaller and less distinguished Lancasterian School was opened at Brown Street (now Brown Street Elementary School, and still in use, though not on the old principle).[19] Its appearance has been spoilt by a nasty cement rendering.

St Patrick's Roman Catholic Church, in Donegall Street, was started in 1810; more or less finished by 1812; but consecrated only in 1815 (Plate 7). The architect was one Patrick Davis, the builder Mr Gaffigan. The rapid increase in the number of Catholic parishioners made it desirable to insert a gallery; the wealthier amongst them objected, on the grounds that the poorer people should continue to go to St Mary's; but the gallery was built all the same.[20] The building of this church, which was demolished in 1875 to make way for the present one, gave rise to some fairly violent controversy on matters of architectural taste in the *Belfast Monthly Magazine*. The building was plainish, but boasted a rudimentary pediment topped by pinnacles and battlements in a vaguely Gothic style. One correspondent objected violently to these: 'Let any one consider how a handsome lady would look, dressed becomingly in every other respect, who to finish her toilet, should clap on her head a grenadier's cap, a judge's wig, a coal-scuttle, or any other preposterous article, and he will have some idea how an incongruous termination may spoil the look of a building, that but for it would have been ornamental to the town'.[21]

An indignant rejoinder appeared soon after, signed 'Nulla Fronti Fides': 'I shall mention the western tower of the CATHEDRAL IN ARMAGH, A CHURCH AT LURGAN, where there is a "pediment" too, and A CHAPEL OF EASE WITHIN THE PRECINCTS OF DUBLIN CASTLE, built by—Johnston, esq., an eminent architect and lately finished. These and hundreds more which I have seen in Great Britain and Ireland have all "embattled Parapets!"' [22] It is at any rate evident from this exchange that there was a livelier awareness of architecture amongst the inhabitants at that time than during many periods since.

***   Amongst the major enterprises of these years was the building of the Academical Institution in College Square. Work was to have begun in 1807, but was deferred due to the high price of timber. The building was actually finished in 1814, more or less to plans prepared by Sir

---

[18]   *Belfast Monthly Magazine*, May 1812.
[19]   Surprisingly, this building—though now surrounded by new houses—is still there, not in too bad order, and being put to good use by Shankill Community Projects Ltd.
[20]   James O'Laverty, *op. cit.*, Vol. II, p. 419. See also the account and photograph of this building in B. M. Walker and Hugh Dixon, *In Belfast Town* (Belfast, 1984), p. 35.
[21]   *Belfast Monthly Magazine*, March 1811.   [22]   *Ibid.*, July 1811.

John Soane, under the supervision first of John McCutcheon, then of James Boyd (Plate 14). It is a question of some difficulty how far the present building can fairly be attributed to Soane.[23] No less than forty-six of the original drawings he prepared in 1807-8, some of them very elaborate, survive in the Soane Museum. But none bears more than the remotest relationship to the buildings actually erected. The costs of the colonnades and quadrangles he laid out far exceeded the means of the Managers, even though Soane gave his services free. It does seem clear, however, that by August 1809 he had prepared revised 'drawings for the workmen'; and in October he wrote, 'I have endeavoured to attend to economy to the utmost of my power and have accordingly substituted piers and arches for columns in different places: other alterations can likewise be made on the same principle'.[24] These plans are now lost; on the whole it seems a reasonable inference that the present building is based on them.

The vista up Wellington Place is closed by the school's three-storey block of dusky brickwork relieved by four pairs of plain stucco pilasters. The round-headed windows on the ground floor are recessed; the only ornament is the deeply recessed and rather heavy pillared porch. Above this, until 1959, was a vacant niche; due to damp, this has been replaced by a round-headed window, which has removed a much-needed plastic feature from the design and substituted a flatly linear one. The back of the original building is now masked by a squat boiler-house from which fat black snake-pipes uncoil round the walls.

The north wing was added, almost certainly to the original plans, in 1834, and is entirely congruous. The Common Hall [25] was built in 1878 to the plans of Thomas Jackson & Son; the West Block was added in 1915 by Watt, Tulloch and Fitzsimons, and extended in 1932 by R. H. Gibson. The Dining Hall (1957) and Science block (1958) are both by Samuel Stevenson & Sons. None of the additions give offence. The same cannot be said of the raspberry-coloured backside turned on the school by the Technical College; see page 71. The buildings are surrounded by reasonable greenery and open space, which will look much handsomer if the young trees get a chance to survive into maturity.

Other public buildings erected about this time include the nearby House of Correction in Fisherwick Place—a mysterious and Piranesian building, labelled over the gateway 'Within Amend, Without Beware'; the date of its erection is given variously as 1803, 1814, and 1817; the date of its demolition seems equally uncertain. A General Hospital was built in Frederick Street in 1815, to designs by a Mr Blain, a three-storey brick building, with a Venetian window above a pedimented porch, which remained in use until 1902.

Far more important was the building in High Street, in 1816, of St George's Church ✱✱✱ (originally named for King George III, but ultimately consecrated in the name of the saint).[26] There are three separate elements in this strange, and in parts superb, church, whose architect was John Bowden, the author of the admirable court-house in Londonderry, and of St Stephen's, Dublin (commonly known as the pepper-pot church). He designed a plain and charming preaching-house to sit modestly behind the tremendous portico (Plate

---

23 Four drawings still in the possession of the school show that the present design is, in fact, based on Soane's work. See Hugh Dixon, *Soane and the Belfast Academical Institution* (Dublin, 1976). 24 Papers and drawings in Sir John Soane's Museum, London. 25 Demolished. 26 'Belfastiensis' scrapbook, Linen Hall Library, Belfast. Badly damaged by bombs on several occasions, its side-wall, not originally intended to be seen, is now opened up to the public gaze: the rather crude patching of the ashlar with cement, in consequence, all too evident. The fine old gate-pillars and railings, mangled by bombs, have unhappily not been worthily replaced. The beleaguered church has succumbed to the insidious temptation to allow cars to use its gravel for week-day parking: so that its augustan façade appears constantly cluttered and besieged.

10). This came from Ballyscullion House, Co. Derry, the second of the three palaces which the Earl-Bishop of Derry built for himself. Whether he planned it himself, or whether it was the work of one of the many architects he patronized, does not seem to be known with certainty. Placido Columbani, a Milanese architect who worked in England, may have had some hand in his previous Irish palace, Downhill.[27] According to a contemporary account of Ballyscullion in the *Belfast News Letter*, 'The general idea of the house was taken from a circular one at Bellisle island in the Windermeer lake, was immediately adopted and communicated to Mr Michael Shanaghan, architect, at Corke, who arranged the present building at Ballyscullion, and committed the inspection of it to Mr D. McBlain, son to the builder of the beautiful spire at Hillsborough—a young man who joining spirit, assiduity and talents to activity gives promise of out-stripping the foremost architects in this Kingdom.'[28] Presumably this is the same young man whose only other recorded achievement in Belfast was the General Hospital. The Bishop lost interest in the house, which was never completed; it was dismantled, ten years after his death, in 1813. The whole facade was bought from his executors by Bishop Alexander, and transplanted to St George's.

Set a little back from the building line of High Street, and partly masked by dusty trees, it is a splendidly dignified example of Georgian stonework at its best. The pediment, now bearing the arms of the see of Down and the town of Belfast in place of its original plaques, is borne on great Corinthian columns and pilasters. The curved front wall, with inset niches, though very elegant, seems slightly odd: Ballyscullion (like its successor, Ickworth, which has a not dissimilar portico) was built as a domed rotunda, of whose outer crust this is a segment.

Inside, however, the church's plain proportions, no doubt very effective when it was first built, have been completely upset. Only the box-pews and gallery, the latter borne on very attractive small acanthus columns, carry any conviction. The original ceiling was plain and low; but unfortunately the roof timbers above it were first exposed, and then encased in polished fir, to the plans of W. J. Barre, after his death in 1867, by the Ecclesiatical Commissioners.[29] This was a bad mistake. Attempts to remedy it by repainting the roof-timbers in white, green, red and gold have only made matters worse. The result is now utterly distracting; the only possible solution would be the restoration of the original low ceiling.

A good deal of money and rather less ingenuity have been spent on Victorian and post-Victorian attempts to cheer up the chancel. There is some atrocious stained glass; a riot of khaki-tinted gilding; and several large murals by Alexander Gibbs (who helped to decorate Keble College Chapel) of which only the two large square panels—the Entry into Jerusalem, and the Via Dolorosa—improve on closer acquaintance. There is an inappropriate plain wooden cross on the West wall.

There is also a strange memorial (1861) to Sir Henry Pottinger, Bart (known to the Chinese during the Opium War as Po, according to Arthur Waley), which says that

ON COMPLETING HIS SUCCESSFUL TREATY WITH CHINA IN 1842

HE WAS DESTINED FOR THE PEERAGE

BY HER GRACIOUS MAJESTY QUEEN VICTORIA THE FIRST

BUT LOST THIS HIGH DISTINCTION THROUGH THE SAME HOSTILE INFLUENCE

[27] Letter from C. J. Robb, *Belfast News Letter*, 18 February 1944; but see P. Rankin, *Irish building ventures of the Earl Bishop of Derry* (U.A.H.S., Belfast, 1972).
[28] *Belfast News Letter*, 14-18 September 1787: quoted by T. G. F. Patterson, *Quarterly Bulletin*, Irish Georgian Society, 1966, p. 77.
[29] Durham Dunlop, *Life of W. J. Barre* (Belfast, 1868), p. 60.

WHICH WAS EXERTED IN VAIN TO PREVENT PARLIAMENT REWARDING
HIS EMINENT SERVICES TO THE STATE.

The exterior of St George's is magnificent by any standards; the inside is rather pathetic, though its respectable antiquity and its associations lend it an atmosphere which St Anne's Cathedral, for example, entirely lacks. It is a strange coincidence that Belfast should contain on the one hand an oval church of the 1780s with a later façade; and on the other, a curved façade of the 1780s tacked on to a later church. We shall know that the ecumenical movement has really arrived when the Rector of Saint George's offers to swap porticoes with the Minister of the First Presbyterian Church in Rosemary Street.

One other notable public edifice dates from the first quarter of the century; the Commercial *** Buildings in Waring Street, built in 1822.[30] The contracting architect was John McCutcheon, but the front looks as though it ought to be attributed to a more sophisticated designer. A splendid formal building of granite, well proportioned, well executed, and above all, well placed to close the vista down Donegall Street, its facade of round-headed windows set between thumping Ionic engaged columns is exceedingly impressive (Plate 15). Above the windows on the *piano nobile* are panels with carved stone swags, trophies and coats of arms. The building has been, on the whole, well restored after war damage; but suffered also from its earlier conversion to a printing press. The roof-line is bulbous with ill-considered protuberances. The large and noble lady designed to recline on top of the parapet has disappeared, if indeed she was ever erected; her two lesser sisters above the doorways are likewise absent. Worst of all, the owners have ignored the neighbourly if servile gestures of Arnott's post-war buildings in Bridge Street, so carefully designed to harmonise with the Commercial Buildings, by adding in 1958 a disastrous garage as sandwich filling between the two; the roof-line is wrong, the window spacing is wrong, there is not even a corresponding string-course; nothing to relate the new to the old but a plain concrete beam in the ugliest place. However, despite all the wrongs committed to it, the building survives—at least, its front does—with real dignity.

The Commercial Buildings provided 'an excellent commercial hotel, a spacious and handsome news-room, and behind these an area with a piazza for the use of the merchants . . . who . . . assemble in the news-room and hold Change on Monday, Wednesday, and Friday.'[31] Indeed, Belfast as an industrial city is not a product of the Victorian age at all; alone in Ireland, it shared in the earliest stages of the Industrial Revolution. In 1800, no less than 27,000 people in and near Belfast were employed in the cotton mills; by 1837, there were 21 cotton factories in the town and neighbourhood, the buildings 'mostly of very large dimensions, six to eight storeys in height'; in some of them, 800 to 2,000 people were employed.[32] No cotton mill of this period survives, but there still exists a detailed description [33] of the flat-roofed and entirely functional mill opened by McCrum Leppers & Co., near the Poorhouse, in 1810. This building, planned and erected by Horatio Barton of Manchester, was covered by a single flat roof 196 feet long by 38 feet broad; the separate steam-engine and boiler-house had a concave roof, designed to be used as a tank for rain water to feed the boiler; every floor had central heating and was carefully ventilated; and the entire factory was lit by gas—thirteen years before the opening of the Belfast gasworks,

[30] See the article by Paul Larmour, and especially the conjectural ground plan of this building, *Ulster Architect*, April 1985, p. 5. Presently in a very ill-kempt state, and long overdue for some loving care and attention.
[31] Samuel Lewis, *op. cit.*, Vol. I., p. 196.   [32] *Ibid.*, p. 194.
[33] *Belfast Monthly Magazine*, February 1810.

itself one of the first in Britain.

On 1 September 1823, after an unfortunate false start the previous night, a handsome pillar in High Street was for the first time surmounted by a six-foot coronet of flame, so brilliant that 'a letter was read by it near the quay, 60 yards distant from the pillar'. The original Gas Works on the Ormeau Road site (now demolished; see page 60) was designed by Mr Barlow, a partner in the Belfast Gas Works Company, and seems to have been a chastely classical parallelogram of buildings: the arched gateway, ornamented with a Doric entablature of cut stone, was supported by pairs of columns; the Clerk's and Engineer's offices each had Doric pediments; the very Retort House had a 'Doric Portico, elevated by a flight of five steps and finished with coping, string course and plinth of cut stone.[34]

The linen mills of this period—for linen gradually superseded cotton during the 1820s and 1830s—have likewise for the most part disappeared. One pleasant example of vernacular
* Georgian industrial architecture, however, is the façade of the Durham Street Weaving Company, in the street of that name.[35] The central gateway with its pediment, niches and garlands of interwoven oak sprays, bearing the date 1834, is naïve but extremely pleasing (Plate 17). On either side of it are ranged two-storey blocks—stone below, brick above—of Georgian character; and a second gateway, with supporting doorways and strong stone voussoirs, though it bears the date 1870, is entirely in keeping with the Georgian original.

The textile trade brought in its wake a need for iron-foundries primarily to supply textile machinery. The first opened in 1792; a number of others over the next few years. Macadam's Soho Foundry, opened in Townsend Street about 1834, is still partly standing; the street front is another fine example of the vernacular classical style. It has a simple monumental brick façade, designed to impress with the strength and solidity of the manufacture. The lower windows to the street are blank, the upper ones heavily pedimented, all admirably proportioned. The gateway is flanked by enormous (and very practical) iron bollards. Later on, this factory participated in the Victorian boom in prefabricated ironwork; and in 1849 exported to Cairo a set of large cast-iron windows for the palace of an Egyptian prince.[36]

Other survivals of the industrial expansion of these years are the Clarendon No. 1 and No. 2 graving docks—the former started in 1796, finished in 1800 (Plate 1); the latter completed in 1826—both of which are still in use.[37] No trace remains of the shipyard established by William Ritchie, an Ayrshireman, in 1792. The port of Belfast has been so completely redeveloped in the course of expansion that hardly a building remains earlier than the 1850s. But there are still a number of warehouses with a nautical flavour. The store of G. Heyn & Sons Ltd,[38] in Garmoyle Street, with its enormously tall and wide doorway, must date from this period.

A particularly fine example was Banquet Buildings, in Victoria Square, built about 1833; demolished 1961. The whole building, five storeys of mellow brick relieved by custardy

---

[34] *Belfast News Letter*, 2 September 1823.   [35] Bombed, and demolished.
[36] H.-R. Hitchcock, *Early Victorian Architecture* (London, 1954), p. 527. None of the more imposing parts of the foundry survive.
[37] D. J. Owen, *Short History of Port of Belfast* (Belfast, 1917), p. 83. These graving docks, now rather unhappily overshadowed by the modern Harbour Office extension, by an intrusive wireless-mast-cum-lamp-standard, and by acres of car and lorry parking and loading space, are still intact, although Clarendon No 1 is now disused, and No 2 only used for the repair of lights, buoys, and such-like. They would provide an ideal home for a maritime museum: especially if H.M.S. Caroline, the only surviving cruiser from the battle of Jutland (moored a few hundred yards away, used by the R.N.V.R.) could be associated with the site.
[38] Demolished.

stucco, was constructed on the slant (Plate 31). The cornerposts of the door were ships'
cannon; the floors were supported on enormous timbers, mostly oak, with the air of the
'tweendecks of a Napoleonic man of war. The front wall was carried up to a peaked gable
where a complex of massive beams bore the pulley-gear. The casks of Banquet Bouquet
whiskey (hence the name) were protected from tipplers not only by heavy iron grilles let
into the woodwork of the unglazed windows but also by iron shutters on the inside.

There is a rather similar, but very dingy, warehouse at 41 and 41a Donegall Quay,
encumbered however with ugly placards and inappropriately painted. Good vernacular
warehouses of this kind, which used to be not uncommon in Belfast, have been disappearing
very fast during the 1960s; they include an elegant pedimented block at 19-23 Franklin Street,
built by Adam McClean in 1835; and a tall slim pilastered warehouse, Caruth's, at 4-6
Marlborough Street, of about the same date. Others have been altered to suit the needs of
modern commerce, and thereby lost all charm: Robert Wilson's, at 20-6 Great Patrick Street,
and 52 York Street, both fall into this class. Others again have been saved by modernization:
10, Hill Street [39] is now the Harp pub, has been very pleasantly repainted, and looks very
handsome. The former tanyard behind the archway at 37 Donegall Street is still attractive;
there is a kind of counting-house at 15 Talbot Street,[40] with a naïve Doric portico and a
bastard too-tall pediment; and there is still a series of warehouses [41] in Commercial Court
off Donegall Street, one of them with a door [42] complete with letter-box in mid-air: pigeon
post, perhaps?.

No early shop-fronts are to be seen in Belfast; even the pubs have survived little better.
Until quite recently, customers were content with traditional surroundings; but lounges,
formica, and fancy lighting have almost ousted the immemorial snugs of Belfast. There are
still a few pleasant exteriors: the Duke of York,[43] in Commercial Court, snuggles gaily
down its atmospheric alleyway; the Liverpool House, at 44 Donegall Quay, a haunt of
departing travellers and their friends, has an outside comfortingly garish with white wall,
black pilasters, quoins and architraves, and plenty of red and yellow ornament.

Offices of this period were indistinguishable outside from dwelling-houses. Henry-Russell
Hitchcock, in his monumental work on *Early Victorian Architecture,* quotes one Edward
I'Anson as saying that the first building designed expressly and solely for use as offices was
built in Clement's Lane, London, in 1823.[44] The accounts of Messrs Ramsay & Garrett,
attorneys, show that in 1813 they paid Thomas Price, carpenter, the sum of £573 19s 9d for
a new office building in York Street, Belfast, unfortunately destroyed in the blitz.[45] Other
early offices may survive unsuspected behind terrace facades.

Georgian terraces continued to be built right up to, and indeed for a considerable time
after, Queen Victoria's accession to the throne. A large number of these are still standing,
though few will stand much longer. Many good examples are to be found in the area of Great
George's Street, the finest being numbers 10-18,[46] which, uncared-for and half-ruinous as   **
they are, have still an opulent dignity. It is very evident, however, from their low-slung
proportions that they were built as merchants' houses and not for the gentry. Each of these
three-storey brick houses has a wide doorway with shallow fluting in the coved arches; the
end ones have Doric pillars and fine fanlights: 12 has elaborate half-fluted Ionic pillars,
with a floral stucco ornament on the lintel, and the old—perhaps the original?—roundel

[39] Still there, but very derelict.   [40] Disappeared.   [41] Gone: mostly bombed.   [42] Flown.
[43] Bombed, demolished, and most unworthily replaced. [44] H.-R Hitchcock, *op. cit.*, p. 375.
[45] Account book in possession of L'Estrange & Brett, Belfast (copy in PRONI, ref. MIC 167).
[46] Still standing, just, but only No. 10 still occupied; the others derelict.

door. All have built-in bootscrapers beside the doorcases, and date from about 1825, though stylistically so late a date is barely credible. In the same street, 36 and 38 are rather earlier, built in 1819, an unusual pair sharing a single roof, one three-storeyed, the other with an extra storey crammed in under the eaves, resulting in some very eccentric window-spacing; numbers 6, 8,[47] 61, 63, and 86 to 94 are less imposing but still good. Other terrace houses nearby of the same period are to be found in Great and Little Patrick Streets; Lancaster Street; Little York Street; Caroline Street; Tomb Street, and Gamble Street.[48]

A much more genteel group of terraces grew up in the 1820s and '30s around the Academical Institution. 1-6, 8 and 9 College Square North,[49] good tall brick houses of the highest quality, date from this period; the balcony of 1 is the finest piece of ironwork in Belfast (Plate 49); 3 has a delightful fanlight of hearts; 8 and 9 have formal projecting Ionic porticoes. A very fine large terrace in Murray Street was demolished between the wars; more buildings of the same series were demolished in College Square East in 1965. The very tall stucco houses beside the Great Northern Railway Station in Great Victoria Street, now used as administrative offices, were built about 1835, by one 'Infant' Graham, seven feet tall, as dwellings; but proved, like their author, over-large.[50] There are some rather less pretentious examples in King Street.

Gradually, good brickwork gave way to sleazy stucco—at any rate, stucco that quickly becomes sleazy if its sparkle is not kept alive by frequent repainting. The meeting-point is exemplified by 7, 9 and 11 Wellington Place, three houses built by Adam McClean in 1830,[51] of which the central one has regency stucco bows; its neighbours are of brick, with formal Ionic porticoes. 7 has rather fine if heavy plasterwork in the entrance and mezzanine hall. 11 had until recently a dingy mirror so placed that, in theory at least, an aerial view of the visitor on the doormat might be reflected through the fanlight to the cowering householder. 10-12 College Square North date from about 1835, fine tall stucco houses; incredibly, the seven enchanting little two-storey mid-Georgian houses in College Place North [52] cannot be earlier than 1832; tucked away in the shadow of the flour-mill, they are real jewels, with glazing-bars all intact, 3 and 5 with their original fanlights, and 6-10 with wide shuttered windows. Another fine but now dingy terrace of this period is to be seen * at 100-6 York Street;[53] each house has a heavy Ionic portico: two are ornamented with arabesques, two with mythological ornament—including a centaur, and Arion riding on his dolphin—rather crudely executed in plaster.

Almost every town dwelling built in the 1820s formed part of a terrace. One of the very few exceptions is St Patrick's Presbytery at 199 Donegall Street (originally the bishop's palace) a handsome box-like three storey brick house in the country rectory tradition. It has a rather naïve doorcase of Ionic pillars, a fanlight, and a truly remarkable (modern) brass front door.

---

[47] Nos 6 and 8 still standing but derelict; all the others demolished (why?).
[48] Almost all of these have been demolished: there are a few lonely survivors in Lancaster Street and Tomb Street.
[49] This street was something of a bomb-alley in the early 1970s: only the Institute for the Deaf, the old Museum, and Nos. 9 to 12, are still standing intact on the north side—all the rest have been bombed. The elegant ironwork balcony of No. 1 was generously presented to the author by Messrs Fitzpatrick after their bomb, and is in safe-keeping for re-erection when the right place and occasion present themselves.
[50] J. J. Marshall, Scrapbook, Linen Hall Library, Belfast.
[51] Lease to A. McClean, 17 August 1829.
[52] Now derelict after many bombs in the vicinity.   [53] Demolished.

On the other side of the church is St Patrick's (now Christian Brothers') School, Donegall   *
Street, opened in 1828. Though still in use, it is a grimy and neglected building, with many
broken windows stuffed with cardboard. Despite its present unkempt appearance,[54] it is
rather a fine exercise in Georgian Tudor; an effective and massive three-storey building
of now blackened brick, with pleasing doorcases and windows. The side view from Donegall
Lane, as glimpsed above a high wall topped with barbed wire, gives a sudden breath of
Hampton Court, with its pointed windows, glazing bars and Tudor dripstone. At its
foundation, the crowd gave three cheers for the success of the undertaking, three for old
Ireland, and three for Dan O'Connell.[55]

Architectural taste in Belfast at the end of the 1820s was becoming more sophisticated,
more various, and more subject to outside influences. The next few years saw ventures not
only in the Tudor, but also in the Greek Revival and the Palladian styles.

One of the most satisfying of these is the May Street Presbyterian Church, built in 1829   **
to the designs of W. Smith. Both inside and outside, it is a really handsome Palladian example
of the Presbyterian taste for the solidly classical. There is a fine brick and stucco pedimented
façade, with a recessed central entrance bay between 'Scamozzian Ionic' columns and
pilasters arranged *in antis*. The contrasting patterns of painted stucco architraves and the
ripe brickwork are beautifully judged, though the church would look better if the stucco
were painted paler and oftener.

Inside, there are twin curving staircases leading to a fine horseshoe gallery of polished
mahogany, carried on cast-iron columns (also Scamozzian); excellent solid curving box-
pews both on floor and gallery; and a good coffered timber ceiling, not over-ornamented
though it dates only from 1872. The memorial doorway to Dr Cooke, for whom the church
was built, is uncommonly good of its period; it was designed in 1872 by John Boyd, architect,
at a cost of £380. The medallion is by the Dublin Sculptor John Foley, RA, who executed
the statue of Albert himself for the Albert Memorial in Hyde Park.[56]

The Belfast Savings Bank[57] in King Street was also completed in 1829; and also,
apparently, by William Smith. It is a rather squat and unsatisfactory building on the whole;
the pediment is a bit too shallow, the windows are too close together, and those on the upper
floor have the architectural equivalent of bushy eyebrows. Nevertheless, its two-storey stucco
façade, rusticated on the ground floor, and with a pleasant shallow porch of coupled Ionic
columns, has a certain clumsy charm. The large room upstairs was stipulated for, and paid
for, as a music-room by the Belfast Anacreontic Society.[58]

It is hard to decide which is the more credible: that this is the work of the W. Smith who,
in the same year, built the excellent May Street Church; or that there were in 1829 two
architects called W. Smith working in Belfast. The name seldom recurs. The Lying-in
Hospital, opened on the Antrim Road in 1830, demolished in 1904, a plain stucco box, was

[54]   Still unkempt, but still there.
[55]   James O'Laverty, *op. cit.*, Vol. II, p. 421. In fact St Mary's, Greencastle, was in 1967 the oldest
Roman Catholic church in the city, consecrated in 1831: now disused, it is a very simple little Gothic
building overlooking the Lough, of red sandstone rendered; it has twin pinnacles over a raised south
window-gable, and a curved stone exterior staircase leading to the gallery. Inexcusably, in my author's
note to the second impression, I confused it with St Mary's Star of the Sea, Whitehouse.

[56]   John Williamson, *May Street Church Centenary* (Belfast, 1929), *passim*.
[57]   Repeatedly damaged by fire and bomb; the porch amputated; finally demolished; now a
car-park.
[58]   W. E. Tyrell, *History of Belfast Savings Bank* (Belfast, 1946) pp 38-40.

by W. Smith,[59] and the Doric Wesleyan Church opened in Linenhall Street, Londonderry, in 1835, is attributed to 'Mr Smyth' of Belfast.[60] Perhaps the May Street Church was the only flash in his pan.

1829 also saw the completion of the Belfast Lunatic Asylum in the 'healthy air' of the Falls Road, then a mile west of the town. This was the only building ever erected in Belfast to the plans of the distinguished Dublin architect, Francis Johnston (1760-1829). Very charming colour-washed elevations, dated 12 March 1827 and bearing the names both of Francis Johnston and of his cousin, partner and successor William Murray (the architect responsible for a number of terraces in Georgian Armagh) may be seen in the National Library in Dublin [61] (Plate 13). Johnston died in 1829, and the plans were in fact probably executed by Murray. Uniform buildings from the same drawings were apparently built in the same year in Londonderry and Armagh.[62] In Belfast, however, the plans do not appear to have been closely followed; the central block with its elegant cupola was erected; but a more pompous porch seems to have been substituted and the windows were altered. In the original drawings, twenty-six narrow cells with arched roofs were to be provided for the more gravely afflicted behind a long colonnade of Doric columns; the convalescents were to be accommodated in wards above. In fact, the colonnade seems never to have been built, and the window sizes seem to indicate that further wards were substituted for some, at least, of the ground-floor cells. Notwithstanding these variations, it is a pity that a building of so much distinction should have been demolished in 1924 by the lunatics of Belfast. The Hospital for Sick Children now stands on its site.

** Two years later, the Greek Revival, the Hellenism of Adam, and of Stewart and Revett, hit Belfast: and with a bang. The Old Museum [63] at 7 College Square North, the first museum in Ireland founded by voluntary subscriptions, was built in 1831 by Messrs Duff and Jackson. According to Pilson, who wrote only fifteen years later, 'the lower storey of this chaste and classic edifice is an imitation of the Choragic Monument of Thrasyllus, with a portico which is an exact copy of that of the octagon tower of Andronicus at Athens; the upper portions after the model of the Temple of Minerva'.[64] Writers of Pilson's period harp a good deal on the chastity of the buildings they admire; it is pleasant to record that here is one which has been neither raped nor seduced in a life of 135 years. It is an admirable four-storey stucco building, all the details (down even to the ventilating grilles) well executed; and still principally used as the resort of learned societies. It is a pity, however, that its paintwork is a little gloomy; however impractical it may seem, a building of so much merit deserves regular coats of white, or.at least cream, paint if it is to keep its sparkle. The top floor contains a delightfully airy room, lit by three windows and three dome-lights; and surrounded by a railed gallery, to which access is obtained up a curling staircase threaded through a bay supported on three pairs of acanthus-capitalled columns. The ironwork both of stairs and balcony is unusual and elegant.

[59] A. G. Malcolm, *History of the General Hospital, Belfast* (Belfast, 1851) p. 45.
[60] *Ordnance Survey of Co. Londonderry* (Dublin, 1837), p. 109.
[61] Currently in the Irish Architectural Archive, Merrion Square, Dublin.
[62] John Betjeman, Article on Francis Johnston in *The Pavilion*, 1946.
[63] Still standing, but in poor condition after many bombs in the close vicinity; the three dome-lights in the top-floor room were very unfortunately roofed in during repairs. Happily, a major restoration programme is, at the date of writing, just about to be undertaken by its owner, the long-established Belfast Natural History and Philosophical Society.
[64] J. A. Pilson, *History of Belfast* (Belfast 1846), p. 38.

The achievement is all the more surprising since Thomas Jackson, as he demonstrated fifteen years later in St Malachy's Church, was far more at home in the Tudor style; while his partner Thomas Duff, whose practice lay principally in South Down, likewise favoured the Tudor style when he built Narrowwater Castle between 1831 and 1837; the Gothic style in his Newry churches; and the Egyptian for the Ross obelisk at Restrevor.[65] On the other hand, Duff seems to have been the author of the Fisherwick Place Presbyterian Church, an Ionic building completed in 1827,[66] and demolished before 1900 to make way for the Assembly's Building.

An even more surprising feat in the Greek Revival style was the very pure Hellenism of the Third Presbyterian Church in Rosemary Street,[67] completed in 1831 and destroyed in the blitz. The four Doric columns of the porch were cast metal, weighing two tons each, produced in Boyd's Belfast Foundry. Its author was 'a native and resident architect', one John Millar, who designed the church while still a student: but shortly after its completion emigrated to New Zealand, then to Australia, and then to New Zealand again, where he died in 1876.

One other fine example of late Georgian classicism was built during this period: Christ   **
Church, in College Square North.[68] There is a monumental simplicity about the stone Ionic front, unpedimented, of this brick church, which was completed in 1833 by William Farrell, the Dublin architect principally responsible for Colebrooke, Co. Fermanagh, and for the completion of Portaferry House, Co Down. The interior is admirably proportioned, and only modestly ornamented. The gallery on three sides is carried on delicate cast-iron columns and brackets. There are pleasant low box-pews. The original segmental ceiling was removed in 1878 when William Batt renovated the church, added a cornice, and 'entirely altered' the windows: but the building has none of that *restored* feeling. There is a weird and impressive three-decker pulpit made of pitch-pine, of probably unique design, dating from 1878 and also the work of William Batt (Plate 63).

---

65 *Archaeological Survey of County Down* (Belfast, 1966), pp 331, 350, 377, 435.
66 J. Huband Smith, *Belfast and its Environs* (Dublin, 1853), p. 30; and see B. M. Walker and Hugh Dixon, *In Belfast Town* (Belfast, 1984), p. 50.
67 J. W. Kernohan, *Rosemary Street Presbyterian Church* (Belfast, 1923) p. 46. When it was blitzed in 1941, a six-foot slab of slate (now in the library of the Presbyterian Assembly) was discovered inside one of the cast-iron pillars of the portico. The inscription reads: "POSTERITY know ye that I a son of dust do cause this tablet to be here inserted that you may not attribute the design of this Building to others than myself which I designed in my Eighteenth year and third of my studentship 1829 During an absence from my native town Belfast the superintendency was entrusted at its commencement to two quacks Duff and Jackson self-styled architects who so mutilated my designs as to make me almost disown them that portion of the dross you People of refined taste which i can foresee you must be can easily distinguish from the refined on my return i fostered my own child untill it grew to what you now behold having began and finished the Peripteral Portico under my own personal superintendance in the year 1831 JOHN MILLAR ARCHITECT". Millar was trained by Thomas Hopper, architect of Gosford Castle. Hugh Dixon, *Ulster Architecture 1800-1900* (U.A.H.S., Belfast 1972), p. 9.
68 J. F. MacNeice, *The Church of Ireland in Belfast* (Belfast, 1931) p. 11; *Irish Builder*, 1878, p. 358. Despite eleven bombs, two arson attacks, and a dwindling congregation, the church survives valiantly. Its exterior looks terrible, with stonework fractured or rendered, and windows boarded up. In contrast, the interior of nave and chancel have been admirably restored, as has the very fine pitch-pine ceiling; and the pulpit is in good shape. Vandals have smashed the toes and fingers of the memorial by S. F. Lynn to Elizabeth Helen Lanyon (d. 1858) wife of Charles Lanyon. The Robson organ deserves restoration. If only the hideously wrecked office block opposite, empty and unrepaired for a full decade, could be demolished! On reconsideration, three stars for Christ Church.

It is just worth mentioning the former Seceders' Church at 9 Alfred Street,[69] built in
1837. It has now been stripped of its portico, and so subdivided that it is impossible to do
more than guess at its original character, housing as it does motor accessories and an optical
works. It seems once, however, to have enjoyed a certain distinction. In the cellars where
the congregation used to stable their horses during service, there is still a sixty-four-feet-
deep well.

Curiously, though the major stylistic streams of contemporary English architecture crossed
the Irish Sea, Belfast is more or less devoid of 'Regency' houses, as that term is usually
used in its Brighton-Cheltenham-bowfront connotations. There are it is true a certain number
of suburban villas engulfed in the tides of later housing but only very rare town houses of
this type. One example is to be found at the corner of Clonard Street and Oranmore Street,
a handsome blue-painted villa, with a bow at each end, the front broken up by eight tall
pilasters and a fine porch of coupled Ionic marble columns; it is now the headquarters of
the Sisters of St Vincent de Paul. The upper part of another may be seen at 6-10 York
Street;[70] above the glass and vitrolite, the custard-coloured stucco is quite impressive.
Originally this seems to have been part of the large house, offices and stores of the Stevenson
family of linen merchants; the date is indeterminate.

In a slightly different idiom, the large and once-elegant house at 3 Hamilton Street
(demolished 1962) was built in 1818 as the town residence of the Duke of Abercorn's family.
It had an unusual doorway framed by Roman Ionic columns, and a stone lintel with stucco
bunches of grapes attached. And in a different idiom again is the large stucco town-house
at 50 Gloucester Street,[71] built about 1835, with a rather Egyptian motif on the door-
canopy and heavy architraves; later apparently one of the three adjacent houses personally
and apparently simultaneously occupied by that redoubtable vet, John Boyd Dunlop, inventor
of the pneumatic tyre.

Indeed, this tinge of the Egyptian taste so much favoured by Thomas Hope is useful in
dating the many terraces of these years. The arched fanlight gave way gradually to the
rectangular one: by degrees hoods or canopies, usually supported on console brackets,
protruded out over the doorways; the detailing of the ornament on these brackets often
provides a clue to the date.

The excellent three-storey terrace at 2-14 North Queen Street,[72] erected by the Belfast
Charitable Society, is particularly helpful, since it can be dated precisely to 1 May 1832,
thanks to the Society's minutes, which record that it was resolved that the rents should be
reasonable, and the appearance 'ornamental to the street and neighbourhood'; which it still
is.

The leisurely development of the Georgian terrace house can be studied instructively in
the area around Joy Street, Hamilton Street, and the district known as 'the Markets', most
of which was built in the 1830s and '40s on land reclaimed either from the tide or from the
former dam of the Cromac paper-mill. There are plain brick terraces [73] of great character

[69] Demolished; see illustration in B. M. Walker and Hugh Dixon, *In Belfast Town* (Belfast, 1984),
p. 21.
[70] Bombed, and demolished.   [71] Demolished.
[72] Bomb-damaged and then demolished, more to increase the security of the adjacent police
station than because the damage was unrepairable.
[73] Nos 14 and 16 well restored in 1984 by the Northern Ireland Housing Executive; the scheme
currently extended to include Nos 18 to 26 Joy Street and 37 to 41 Hamilton Street. Unfortunately,
all the rest of the houses mentioned in Joy Street, Sussex Place and Hamilton Street are scheduled
for demolition, if not already gone: with the possible exception of Nos 4 to 12 Joy Street, whose
future is still in doubt.

at 2-32 Joy Street and 4-18 Sussex Place; again at 7-19, 35-41 and 36-46 Hamilton Street (7 has an odd but pleasing massive Norman-Regency pointed doorway); a fine stucco terrace at 20-30 Hamilton Street, set back a few feet from the street line, with hooded doorways, light pilasters, an ornamental frieze, acroteria, and a rusticated ground floor. This district more than any other gives a vivid impression of Belfast as it was before the full gale-force of Victorian industrial expansion struck. Most of the houses are in fair order, respectable, and cared-for by their tenants, if not always by their landlords. It would be well worth preserving at least a selection of them when the time for redevelopment comes. *

In this same district may also be observed the gentle transition from Georgian Gothick to Early Victorian Tudor. 118-124 Joy Street,[74] brick terrace houses like their neighbours, have doorways and windows in the Tudor taste, complete with label dripstones and appropriate fanlights in the upper parts of the ground-floor windows. Still more charming are the delightful terrace houses 130-8 Donegall Pass,[75] likewise built about 1837, with their pointed doorcases and windows, roundel doors, and pretty balconies and fanlights (Plate 16). Originally, these houses stood amongst fruit-gardens on the outskirts of the town. (There is a similar terrace, with ornaments from the same moulds but now irredeemably mutilated, at the opposite outskirt of the then town, at 85-91 Antrim Road.[76])

There was no sudden stylistic leap when Victoria succeeded her uncle William on the throne. Georgian buildings continued to go up, in Ireland as in England, well into the 1850s, '60s, and even '70s; but imperceptibly taste was changing—away from the austerity of the strict Georgian canon; towards the effervescent ornamentation of the full-blooded Victorian era.

[74] All demolished.
[75] Severely bomb-damaged; vandalised beyond repair while plans for their rehabilitation were being concocted; ultimately, alas, demolished.
[76] Repeatedly damaged by fire and other bombs; rightly or wrongly, considered beyond repair; ultimately demolished.

THREE

THE
LOW VICTORIAN ERA

1837—1867

The word 'Victorian' is now applied (often disparagingly) to the products and events of every part of the Queen's long reign. In fact, there was no more a single architectural style throughout those sixty-three years than throughout the years from 1900 to 1963. Indeed, the word came to have a definite meaning during her lifetime; it meant 'in a different architectural style from anything built before'. But during the first thirty years after her accession very little was built that could not easily have been built before.

It is true that many Victorians were heartily sick of the uniformity and tedium of Georgian architecture; this process had started much earlier. In 1810, a writer in the *Belfast Monthly Magazine* had commented revealingly on a tour of North Antrim, 'Dervock consists of one long street, but from the uniformity of its houses, the eye of the traveller is fatigued before he reaches the end of it.' [1] The next hundred years saw an ever-more determined struggle to combat this *fatigue* by substituting richness and variety for the austere proportions that pleased the Georgian eye. 'Rich' was as much the cliché of architectural applause in the 1860s as 'chaste' had been in the 1830s; or as 'clean lines' became in the 1950s. This process, however, did not really gather momentum until Queen Victoria's reign was half over.

The Tudor and Italianate modes became part of the architect's repertoire, it is true; but both had their roots in the Regency. The scholarly Gothic revivalism of A. W. Pugin and the ecclesiologists only took effect gradually, insofar as it took root in Ireland at all. It may be rough and ready, but it is reasonable to draw a line between the Low Victorianism of the years 1837 to 1867, and the High Victorianism of the remaining years of the century. And this line appears surprisingly accurately drawn in Belfast. For 1867 saw the first irruptions into Belfast of the German-Scottische-baronial style, so disastrously [2] introduced in Scotland by David Bryce, so disastrously fostered by Prince Albert till it reached its apogee at Balmoral Castle in 1853. This was the style and this the year when the Albert Memorial at the foot of High Street was completed to plans by W. J. Barre. This was the style and the year also when work started on Belfast Castle, whose plans were ostensibly by Charles Lanyon but probably in fact by his young partner W. H. Lynn. [3] In

---

[1] *Belfast Monthly Magazine*, February 1810.
[2] I no longer feel that the Scottish baronial style was such a disaster: and have come much to admire its better examplars, though there are others which still seem to my eye clumsy and unhappy.
[3] It now appears that the designs for Belfast Castle, though no doubt influenced by Lynn, were

this year, too, there ended once and for all the vicious rivalry which had subsisted between Lanyon and Barre: for Barre died prematurely at the age of thirty-seven. Both had completed all their finest work: several buildings of Barre's were executed posthumously; Lanyon lived on till 1889, but almost all his later work may be attributed to his partners and assistants.

The first years of the new reign gave no hint of what was to come. A very modest small stone church [4] with narrow pointed windows in the regency style, was built for the Church of Ireland in 1838 on the Upper Malone Road; it was for some years used as a church hall by the adjoining Presbyterian congregation of McCracken Memorial. A very plain and dull brick meeting-house was built in 1840 by the Quakers in Frederick Street.[5] Rather more satisfactory was the building in May Street now used as a church by the Plymouth Brethren, but originally built for the Anacreontic Society as the Victoria Music-Hall in 1840. It is a coarse but vigorous exercise in late classical architecture, but somehow not entirely successful. The ironwork and the great slabs of stucco are pleasingly massive; the latter would be more so if the grey-green paint were not continually peeling. A new and inappropriately Conservative superscription was inserted into the façade when the building was converted from impious to pious purposes in 1887: it reads, 'My son fear thou the Lord and the King: and meddle not with them that are given to change.' The Music-Hall seems to have been designed without benefit of architect;[6] the builder was one Peter Lundy, who was also responsible for the very pleasant Royal Terrace, Lisburn Road,[7] built in 1848, largely from the bricks of an earlier brewery on the same site. Unfortunately, Lundy went bankrupt and emigrated hastily to America shortly afterwards.

The Scottish United Secession Presbyterian Church in College Square North [8] (completed in 1843, demolished in 1966), was bleak, grey and defensible, Tudor with a strongly Scottish flavour; the exterior undistinguished, the interior rather charming by reason of the honeycomb of varnished box-pews, particularly well arranged in the double-S of the horseshoe gallery, and the dark high pulpit with twin curving stairs.

Apart from the very many Georgian dwellings which continued to be built for several decades, the finest late-Georgian building in Belfast is St Malachy's Roman Catholic Church   ***
in Alfred Street,[9] completed in 1844 by Thomas Jackson (Plates 18 and 19). It is a superb example of Sir-Walter-Scottery at its most romantic. The exterior, though of rather dingy brick, is fine and dignified, soaring upwards in cruciform to lofty turrets and an oak tower

---

in fact the work of young John Lanyon: see note on page 47.

[4] In fact, designed by William Farrell (drawings in R.C.B., Dublin, Folio 6).

[5] The old Quaker meeting-house, designed by Thomas Jackson, is now derelict, though the new one alongside it survives in a kind of *hortus conclusus* amidst desolate wastelands. See Hugh Dixon, *Proceedings of B.N.H.P.S.*, Vol 9, 1978, p. 28.

[6] The May Street Hall, in fact also designed by Thomas Jackson, was considerably bomb-damaged, and ultimately demolished, as no satisfactory use for it could be found, despite the fact that it had been listed: now a car park. I now much regret its loss, and think I under-rated its merits as an important component in a fine group of good buildings. See Hugh Dixon, *ibid.*

[7] Royal Terrace was regrettably demolished to make way for the Russell Court Hotel, itself in turn wrecked by bombs, now empty and derelict for many years. Thomas Jackson was, again, the original designer; see Hugh Dixon, *ibid.*

[8] This church, yet again by Thomas Jackson, was demolished to make way for the odious eight-storey office block designed for the Youth Employment Service, whose bombed-out wreck still overshadows the whole locality. See Hugh Dixon, *ibid.*

[9] Shaken by many bombs in the surrounding streets, St Malachy's has been well repaired and restored from floor to ceiling. In order to accommodate the new liturgy, the old high altar has been set back in a kind of recess; but this has been discreetly handled, and is not too distressing.

(from which the spire was removed, with advantage; it is said because the tolling of the great bell in it interfered with the satisfactory maturing of the whiskey in Messrs Dunville's adjacent distillery). The interior is enchanting: it is as though a wedding-cake had been turned inside-out, so creamy, lacy and frothy is the plasterwork. The ceiling is fan-vaulted in imitation of Henry VII's chapel in Westminster Abbey. The high altar is placed in one of the short arms of the cross to make more space—an extremely unusual departure from the traditional arrangement. Altar, reredos and pulpit are all pale and delightful. The altarpiece is by one of the Piccioni family, refugees to Belfast from Austrian Italy. Beside it lies the site of the Chapel Fields, now built over, but famous in Belfast folklore, where throughout the slump of the 1930s anyone who could afford 6d could see contests between such figures as Buckus McGahey [10] and the Birdman in Ma Copley's tent.

The 1840s—the Famine years—were, however, a still more miserable period in Belfast. It is true that the greater prosperity of North-East Ireland, the greater security conferred by the Ulster tenant right, and a much greater degree of industrial development, shielded the districts around Belfast from the catastrophic sufferings of the West and South of Ireland. But neither potato blight, nor typhus, nor dysentery, nor relapsing fever, nor cholera, proved to be respecters of tenant right. There had been an acute epidemic of cholera in 1832. Fever was endemic throughout the later 1830s. In 1840 it was resolved at a town meeting that Queen Victoria's marriage should not be celebrated by the customary fireworks and illuminations, but that 'the money which would be expended in this mode of testifying joy should be given to the Treasurer of the Fever Hospital',[11] and £178 was raised in this manner. The new Workhouse, with accommodation for one thousand inmates, was built on the Lisburn Road in 1841. To it was added the new Union Hospital in 1845: 'a model of Hospital architecture . . . estimated to accommodate between 300 and 400 patients'. Both these gloomy buildings of undressed stone, which now constitute the nucleus of the enormously enlarged and modernized Belfast City Hospital, seem to have been built to the standardized plans prepared for use throughout Ireland by the Board of Works in Dublin, under the supervision of Jacob Owen.[12]

But worse was to come. 1847 was marked by 'the prevalence of smallpox and dysentery amongst the poor'. To this was added typhus; an emigrant vessel, the *Swatara*, had sailed from Liverpool with several hundred passengers, but her captain was obliged to put back, once into Derry and twice into Belfast, and to land a large proportion of her passengers there. The epidemic spread fast; the number of cases on 29 May was 1,149; there were 13,676 admissions to hospital before the end of the year. Seven hundred convalescents had to be accommodated in canvas tents in the workhouse grounds. Dr Malcolm, writing only four years later, commented: 'It may be safely affirmed, that one out of every five persons in Belfast was attacked during this year . . . We well remember the aspect of the hordes of poor who thronged into the town, from all parts. Famine was depicted in the look, in the hue, in the voice, and the gait. The food of a nation had been cut off'.[13]

Two years later, there was another outbreak of cholera. In 1852, potato blight was still

[10]   The late Ralph Bossence informed me that "Buckus" should have read "Buckets".
[11]   A. G. Malcolm, *History of the General Hospital, Belfast*, (Belfast, 1851), p. 116.
[12]   The standard design of Union Workhouse employed in Ireland was in fact not that of Jacob Owen, but of the Yorkshire architect George Wilkinson, appointed in 1839 as architect to the Poor Law Commissioners. See M. H. Gould, *The Workhouses of Ulster*, (UAHS, Belfast, 1983), p. 6.
[13]   A. G. Malcolm, *op. cit.*, pp 129-131.

18

Pls. 18 and 19: St Malachy's Roman Catholic Church was planned by Thomas Jackson, then aged 33, in 1840. Both the tall turrets of the exterior and the icing-sugar flamboyance of the interior are superb examples of romantic Sir-Walter-Scottery. Extensively restored; the altar recently recessed in a kind of cavern.

20

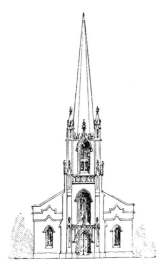

21

Pl. 20: The School for the Deaf and Dumb was designed by the youthful Charles Lanyon in 1843, and demolished in 1963. Pl. 21: Trinity Church, destroyed in the blitz, was a primitive prototype of the Gothic Revival, designed by Lanyon in 1842. Pl. 22: Lanyon made his name with his adaptation of the old Exchange and Assembly Rooms (see Pl. 3) as the head office of the Belfast Bank (now a branch of the Northern Bank). He lovingly preserved Sir Robert Taylor's interior, but encased the exterior in stucco in the Italian palazzo style popularized by Sir Charles Barry.

22

Pl. 23: The Crumlin Road Gaol was completed in 1846, to plans by Lanyon. Pl. 24: The County Courthouse immediately opposite was built, also to Lanyon's designs, in 1850; its exterior was much altered (for the worse) in 1905. Both buildings, which face each other, now surrounded by defensive screens; the Courthouse rather brightly painted but still recognisable; the Gaol so altered after bomb and other attacks, and protective works, as to be now totally unrecognisable.

25

During the 1840s and 1850s
Lanyon adorned Belfast with a
series of noble public buildings.
Pl. 25: The Assembly's College
was opened in 1855. Pl.26: The
Queen's College (now Queen's
University) in 1849. Pl. 27: The
Custom House, a building of
great dignity finished in 1857,
originally stood in the middle of a
wide cobbled piazza.

26

27

28

. 28: In 1868, Lanyon, fighting to retain his
at in Parliament, rashly announced in a
eech at Jennymount: 'And without Egotism I
ay say that the large increase in the
nstituency of Belfast is owing to my
ertions.' He meant to refer to the edifices
ith which he had adorned the town; his
ords were unfortunately open to a less
ifying interpretation, illustrated in this
mpoon, 'A Plumper for Sir Charles'. Pl. 29:
is detailed drawings for the Queen's College
monstrate the delicacy of line of which he
as capable.

29

Warehouse architecture became very much more sophisticated between 183 and 1860. Pl. 31: Banquet Buildings, a whiskey store built about 1833, was a fin example of the robust vernacular style: demolish in 1961 to make way for a multi-storey office block, Churchill House. Pl. 30: I marked contrast is the slim Italianate elegance of the block at 9-15 Bedford Stre built in 1852 probably to plans by Lanyon: demolish in 1970 to make way for a multi-storey office block, Windsor House.

Pl. 32: Lanyon built the heavily rusticated Head Office of the Northern Bank in 1852: (acquired by the Trustee Savings Bank). Notice the Georgian treatment of the attic windows, which are invisible from the street. In the background, the Custom House. Pl. 33: A view of Corporation Square about 1860. Sinclair Seamen's Presbyterian Church (see also Pl. 68) was completed by Lanyon in 1857; the Harbour Office (later much enlarged) by George Smith, the Harbour Engineer, in 1854.

33

34

Pl. 34: The Provincial Bank
of Ireland was one of the last
works of W. J. Barre; it was
completed in 1868, after his
death. Pl. 35: Clanwilliam
House (now Danesfort) was
built by Barre for Samuel
Barbour in 1864. This early
photograph shows it still bare
and naked immediately after
its completion, before lawns
had sprouted or trees been
planted. Now undergoing
extensive restoration.

35

flourishing around Belfast.[14] There followed a gradual recovery. But it is against this background that the series of public buildings erected in Belfast in the forties must be viewed.

Apart from the Workhouse (1841) and the Union Hospital (1845), the series comprised the Queen's Bridge (1843); the School for the Deaf and Dumb (1845); the Prison (1846); the Queen's College (1849); and the County Courthouse (1850). Save for the two first, all of these were the work of a single remarkable young engineer, Charles Lanyon. His is certainly the greatest single name in the development of Belfast; his career would well repay detailed study, for which the available materials are all too scanty.[15]

Born in Sussex in 1813, he was apprenticed to Jacob Owen of the Board of Public Works in Dublin, and (shrewdly and very characteristically) married Owen's daughter. He was first appointed Surveyor of Kildare, but in 1835 obtained a transfer, at his own request, to the more flourishing county of Antrim, of which Belfast then formed part, and continued to hold the post until 1860. In 1836, his twenty-third year, he built the remarkably fine Glendun road viaduct, of local stone. He was associated not only with the engineering of the Antrim coast road, but also with road-making inland: amongst his most beloved achievements are the two avenues of fir trees whose roots bind together the roadway through the bog between Ballymena and Ballymoney.[16]

At the same time, he undertook private commissions, as the conventions of the day allowed. During the thirties, he built several country houses, of which the finest is Drenagh, Limavady, Co. Derry, which he constructed to plans by an unknown architect,[17] drawn up fifty years earlier in the 1780s. The detailing of this handsome classical house, built of well-dressed reddish stone, shows that he started with a clear mastery of Georgian technique. In 1843, for the first time, he was called on to carry out a town job: with another engineer, John Frazer, he was employed to build the new Queen's Bridge more or less on the line of the old Long Bridge. It was greatly admired, and was described three years after its completion as 'truly chaste and commanding'.[18] Its chastity however was violated when, in 1885, a widened footpath was added on cantilevers. The result looks like the flight-deck of an aircraft-carrier, oddly supported on sprouting clumps of columns.

From the point of view of architectural taste, his arrival in Belfast brought a gale of fresh air into the town. He was commissioned by the Church Accommodation Society of the diocese to build the new Trinity church (off Upper Donegall Street; completed 1843; destroyed in the blitz) (Plate 21). The writer of a contemporary *Guide to Belfast and its Environs*, Huband Smith, was bowled off his feet by Lanyon's drawings: 'The design of this church is in the pointed Gothic style; and when complete will at once indicate the purpose for which it has been erected. This object is too often lost sight of in designs for modern churches, where we not unfrequently see the exterior copied, with a monstrous solecism in taste, not to speak of its unfitness on higher grounds, from some pagan temple, or other ancient Greek or Roman secular structure'.[19] Evidently either Mr Lanyon, or Mr Huband

---

[14] Cecil Woodham-Smith, *The Great Hunger*, (London, 1962), p. 407.
[15] Alas, still as scanty in 1985 as in 1966, despite the unsuccessful researches of many individuals: all Charles Lanyon's papers, and most of his drawings, seem to have disappeared without trace.
[16] Known as "The Frosses": in poor shape, and in need of care and inter-planting very soon if they are not to disappear into the bog.
[17] The 'unknown architect' was in fact John Hargrave: See A. J. Rowan, *North-West Ulster*, (London, 1979), p. 249; and W. D. Girvan, *Buildings of North Derry*, (UAHS, Belfast, 1975), pp 21-23; and the date more probably around 1825.
[18] J. A. Pilson, *History of Belfast*, (Belfast, 1846), p. 35. [19] J. Huband Smith, *op. cit.*, p. 41.

Smith, or both, had been reading the publications of the Tractarians.

***   But his reconstruction of the Belfast Bank's headquarters in Waring Street was still more daring. The directors had recently acquired the old Exchange and Assembly Rooms (see page 4); in 1845 they called in Lanyon to refurbish them.

It had been thought fitting since classical times that public buildings should display a dignity emblematic of their functions. The banks were the first public institutions to follow suit, largely as an exercise in public relations. Of the fifty Irish banks registered in 1804, every one is said to have failed.[20] In 1817, T. L. Peacock visualized a Bank as 'a little shop, of which the shutters were closed, with the word BANK in golden letters over the door, and a large board on the central shutter, notifying that "Messieurs Smokeshadow, Airbubble, Hopthetwig and Company find themselves under the disagreeable necessity of suspending their payments".[21] Bank scares—almost unimaginable nowadays (at any rate in Britain)—occurred, with scenes of wild alarm, as late as 1847, 1857, and 1866. No wonder the bankers called in Lanyon and his successors to provide them with a new and more imposing public image. Lanyon chose to encase the exterior of the Exchange in elaborate stucco, in the Italian palazzo style pioneered by Sir Charles Barry. In 1831 Barry had completed the Travellers' Club in Pall Mall, a startling adaptation of Raphael's Pandolfini Palace in Florence. Its plans were published in 1839. Lanyon adopted them with alacrity. He introduced a similar bold cornice, a similar highly-ornamented string-course, and similar aedicules (like miniature houses) around the first-floor windows (Plate 22). This is one of the prototypes—the first in Ireland, so far as I know—of the international Renaissance Revival; the very Raphaelism that led to the later revolt of Pre-Raphaelism. It is also one the handsomest and most satisfactory buildings in Belfast, apart from the faintly ridiculous lantern on the roof. The eye has now become sated with Italianate office blocks of later date and lesser quality; but contemporaries greatly admired Lanyon's work, which came to them all fresh and novel; and with reason. Pilson, writing in 1846, the year after its completion, commented: ' . . . it has been so much altered and beautified as to have undergone a complete metamorphosis from a large pile of unseemly black brick to one of the handsomest architectural ornaments of the town'.[22] Lanyon carefully preserved Sir Robert Taylor's interior so far as was possible; unhappily, in 1895 W. H. Lynn remodelled and renovated the building 'in marked contrast to its previous internal appearance',[23] and no fragment of Taylor's Assembly Rooms can now be detected.[24]

The School for the Deaf and Dumb was likewise opened in 1845, on the Lisburn Road (demolished by Queen's University, 1963) (Plate 20). It was an impressive and, in a way, a remarkable building, of considerable extent. Pilson described it as follows: 'This edifice is composed of English brick, the doors and windows decorated with richly ornamented cut-stone dressings. It is in the Tudor style of architecture, comprising a centre and two wings. The front elevation extends from east to west 222 feet, and the wings at each end 164 feet to the rear. The main building is two stories high, and over the principal entrance rises an elegant, unique, octagonal dome, which has a very pleasing, and, at the same time,

---

20   Sir Robert Peel, 9 June 1845; Hansard, *Parliamentary Debates*, 3rd Series, Vol. LXXXI, Col. 248.
21   T. L. Peacock, *Melincourt*, (London, 1817), chapter XXX.
22   J. A. Pilson, *op. cit.*, p. 37.   23   *Irish Builder*, 1895, p. 215.
24   Now a branch of the Northern Bank; rather unsympathetically painted though well cared for. The dark brown colour chosen for the ground floor is inappropriate in itself, and also has the effect of slicing the building horizontally as though it were a layer-cake.

impressive effect.' [25] Its destruction provoked a modest but creditable outcry; it must however be admitted that its structure was crumbling and somewhat unsound, and that its merits as a piece of scenery exceeded its practical usefulness.[26]

Indeed, there was a little of the stage designer about Lanyon; his imaginative grasp of architectural composition, and in a great variety of styles, was remarkable; the structural soundness of his execution invariably somewhat less so. On the other hand, it must be borne in mind that his best work was all completed during times of acute economic and social strain. It is likely that his clients cared less for durability than for economy. Nevertheless, they insisted that the appearance of each building they commissioned should be congruous with its purpose. Indeed the Early Victorians were incapable—perhaps rightly incapable—of separating function from appearance. Every building, they felt, should wear its heart on its sleeve. A church ought to be Gothic; a school or a college ought to be Tudor; a courthouse ought to be Classical; a bank ought to look like the palace of merchant princes, or at least princely merchants; a prison ought to be grim and frowning.

This the exterior of the Crumlin Road Gaol,[27] completed in 1846, undoubtedly is. There were two schools of thought amongst Victorian architects regarding the style most suitable for prisons. Reading Gaol (by Scott and Moffatt) and Holloway (by J. B. Bunning) adopted with formidable effect the fortress principle; Pentonville, however, built by Sir Charles Barry in 1842, exemplified the Piranesian manner. Not surprisingly, perhaps, in view of his earlier success, Lanyon chose to follow Barry once again. Not only the style, but the radial layout also, closely resemble Barry's work. The entrance block to the prison (originally, the Governor's house) is of heavily rusticated stone in the somewhat sinister manner of Giulio Romano, with columns, pilasters and quoins likewise rusticated, and some of them vermiculated too for good measure (Plate 23). The ironwork in the five wings, and particularly in the central semi-circular hall from which they spring, is impressive.

In 1850 he built the County Courthouse immediately opposite (Plate 24); a corridor beneath the Crumlin Road enables the accused to be wafted discreetly from the one to the other. This is a very large and imposing Corinthian block in stucco; the portico and pediment are reasonably classical, but much of the detailing is in a vaguely Italian Renaissance style. The building was enlarged, and the subtlety of its original façade wholly destroyed, in 1905, to plans by Young and Mackenzie. The pediment is surmounted by a figure of Justice, with the conventional sword and scales, carved by Joseph Kirk, RHA, of Dublin; the latter have had holes punched in them (to let the rain through? to discourage birds nests?) and sway disconcertingly in the wind. The exterior is painted battleship-grey; its appearance, especially from the back where it towers on the slopes above the Old Lodge Road, in itself constitutes a formidable deterrent to evil-doing.[28] Inside, the central hall is not quite large enough for its height, though imposingly planned. The courtrooms are impressive but curious; their internal arrangements give the impression of a cross between an anatomy lecture theatre and a Presbyterian church; there is a honeycomb of grained deal pews, high,

---

[25] J. A. Pilson, *op cit.*, p. 50.
[26] Progress: I do not think it could conceivably have been demolished today. It was the sense of outrage at the destruction, in quick succession, of this building and Queen's Elms (see page 43) that led to the formation of the Ulster Architectural Heritage Society.
[27] Now quite unrecognisable after successive bomb and other attacks, and successive consequent re-fortifications.
[28] Its curtilege, like that of the Gaol, is today heavily, and of necessity, fortified; the building itself has been rather gaudily repainted to look like an orange-cream-cake, in an effort to cheer up a very depressing and down-at-heel environment.

narrow and uncomfortable, raked sharply upwards to the back of each court. The superb cast-iron chandeliers have recently been removed, and modern (and quite appropriate) light fittings substituted.

***   The Queen's College (now Queen's University) in University Road had been opened in the previous year, 1849 (Plates 26 and 29). Although very many buildings have been added (and some substracted) in the immediately surrounding area, the original façade by Lanyon remains unchanged: an extraordinarily harmonious and attractive revival of red-brick Tudor. The central tower is a very accurate translation of the Founder's Tower at Magdalen College, Oxford; this theme is repeated in the lesser towers that break the long and strictly symmetrical facade. The original plans were subjected to much cheese-paring by the Board of Works; neither of the sides, still less the very stark ambulatory at the rear, are as effective as the front. Even from the latter many details were amputated: gargoyles, roof-lanterns, finials, and carved statues were completely omitted; the fascinating range of mock-Elizabethan chimneys shown in the original drawings also, alas. Unfortunate cuts were also made in the accommodation to be provided, which proved in the event foreseeably inadequate. Professors Moody and Beckett, in their history of the University, point out that the president and vice-president were lavishly provided with residential quarters; of the space that remained, a very large proportion was occupied by public halls, lecture-rooms and laboratories; but the accommodation for the students 'amounted precisely to a cloakroom, four water-closets and a row of urinals'.[29]

It must be acknowledged that Queen's, though delightfully designed, was not very well built. The mellow brickwork and slightly crumbly stonework require a great deal of maintenance. Its interior is rather impractical, though some parts, and notably the staircase and gallery leading from the soaring entrance hall to the (now) Vice-Chancellor's office, are extremely fine. Notwithstanding its shortcomings, the old College remains one of the principal ornaments of Belfast; it is to be hoped that, in this instance at least, the University will succeed in mastering the iconoclastic impulses to which it has in recent years been prey.[30]

In the early years of the new reign, Lanyon enjoyed the lion's share of the work that was available. Curiously, however, he does not at this stage in his career seem to have taken a major part in the building of the new railways that were then spreading through Ireland, though in later life a large part of his lucrative engineering practice consisted of railway work. The Great Northern Railway Station [31] opened in Great Victoria Street in 1848, seems to have been the work of John Godwin, the Company's engineer, who, in the following year, became the first Professor of Civil Engineering at the new Queen's College. The pompous façade centres upon the twelve groaning Doric columns of the porch, carrying, however, almost nothing; the real weight of the roof being borne by two slim and inconspicuous iron pillars inside the portico. The interior is a rather incoherent mess of ironwork. The fancy glass awning outside the front is an unhappy afterthought; the wildly inappropriate yellow and black tiles recently added to the outside of the refreshment-room are even more deplorable. The heaviness of the building is accentuated by gloomy battleship-

[29]   T. W. Moody and J. C. Beckett, *Queen's, Belfast, 1845-1949: the History of a University* (London, 1959), Vol. I, p. 115.
[30]   It mostly has. And it must be acknowledged that the University has spent large sums on the refurbishment of its older buildings, and the replacement of important details such as ornamental ridge-tiles and crestings.
[31]   Demolished to make way for the 13-storey Europa, now Forum, Hotel.

grey paint (the captain of any battleship who allowed his command to become equally bedraggled would certainly be cashiered). Though it does not compare with the better contemporary English stations, it must have had a certain modest grandeur before it became befrilled and begrimed.

Smithfield Market, the only other public building of the '40s, is even less imposing. An unimpressive quad of cottage-shops, with covered ways between them, and a central tunnel, it was opened in 1848 on the site of the old Corn and Hide Market to plans by the Borough Surveyor. In it, junk-shops and higgledy-piggledy have ever since congregated very enjoyably. Many attempts have been made to abolish it: in 1892 Charles Lanyon's son John wanted to build here a Central Railway Station with 10½ acres of glass roof, and a great hotel; more recently a central bus station has been proposed. So far it has withstood all assaults.[32]

New dwelling-houses, particularly for the better-off, continued to be built, mainly along the lines of the new Lisburn, Crumlin and Antrim Roads, all opened in the later 1830s. Cliftonville [33] was laid out by Thomas Jackson in the 1840s, a villa estate modelled on Clifton on the outskirts of Bristol. The area near the new Queen's College developed particularly fast. The three delightful little stucco two-storey houses at the entrance to Mount **
Charles,[34] each with a slim Doric portico, date from 1842; University Street was begun in the same year. Upper and Lower Crescents, highly imposing stucco terraces in the Bath manner with Corinthian columns and pilasters rising two full storeys, were put up by an enterprising builder, James Corry, the former in 1846, the latter in 1852; both are now sadly dingy and peeling.[35] The imposing length of University Square, an admirable brick terrace *
lent variety by a miscellany of (mostly charming) later bow-windows and a succession of mature magnolia trees, was started in 1848. Bedford Terrace, the extraordinary little block *
comprising 189-97 Sandy Row, now deplorably shopped, but still proudly displaying a tremendous curly *corniccione* supported on Corinthian pilasters, was built in 1852.[36] These houses and terraces are mostly the work of anonymous builders; all are directly in the Georgian tradition. The 'Victorian' style was slow in working its way down to residential architecture.

---

[32] See *Irish Builder*, 1892, p. 215. More recent assaults were successful. On the night of 6 May 1974, the entire quadrangle and all it contained were burned out by bombers. Under pressure from the displaced shopkeepers, the Council provided them with a discontinuous square of shoddy-looking prefabricated huts, grouped around tarmac and rather wan flower-beds. The result is depressing, the more so as many of the buildings surrounding the square have either been bombed into dereliction or out of existence. The shopkeepers however still value their traditional pitch and their independence, and to date have shown little enthusiasm for the latest ambitious Royal Avenue—Smithfield development scheme.

[33] Numbers 26 to 30 Cliftonville Road, built as a terrace of three tall handsome stuccoed houses with classical detailing in 1831, were later converted into a Home for the Blind; now being restored as flats by the Hearth Housing Association. Thomas Jackson's own house next door, No. 24, was burned to the ground by vandals in 1981.

[34] Of these three houses, No. 2 was badly bombed but has been nicely rebuilt, complete with tall yellow chimney-pots; No. 4 has been knocked about—its Georgian sashes were blown out—but is still there; No. 6 has lost its portico, and is shabbily painted, but still retains its splendid tall single chimney.

[35] Upper and Lower Crescents are in a patchy state; now that the threat of demolition for road-works has receded, some are very run-down, others well cared-for. They well deserve a concerted effort of positive conservation.

[36] This block now looks very strange, after much bomb-damage: all the upper windows have been blocked up and replaced by advertising placards; only the great cornice and the upper halves of the pilasters survive; the building now houses the Crescent Bars.

The development of the town was greatly assisted by the final downfall of the precarious finances of the Donegall family.[37] Somehow the second Marquis had struggled on under his load of debt until his death in 1844. The creditors became more pressing; and in 1850 the whole estate was placed in the hand of the Incumbered Estates Court Commissioners, a body appointed to cut through the impossible tangle of mortgages and borrowings with which almost every estate in Ireland had become encumbered in consequence of the famine. Every property in the town was meticulously mapped and listed.[38] An enormous percentage had to be sold before the claims of all the creditors were satisfied. In consequence, Belfast was converted overnight from a town of tenants with short leases to a town of freeholders. It was an opportune moment, coinciding as it did with the struggle to retore prosperity after the Famine. As Dr Jones remarks in his *Social Geography of Belfast*, 'it is clear that the freeing of the land from the control of the Donegall family had a very great effect on the expansion and the development of the town. It came at an important point in the history of Belfast, and probably contributed as much as the more obvious factors to the rapid increase in rate of building which characterized the second half of the nineteenth century.' [39]

And John Stuart Mill expressed the same view in his *Political Economy*: 'The improvidence of the Donegall family, resulting as it did in the practical alienation of the soil of the town and the adjoining country and the creation of innumerable freehold owners of building ground, did more to promote the rise and progress of Belfast than any other fact or circumstance in its history'.[40]

But neither public building nor church building picked up quickly. The Methodist Church in Donegall Square East, having been completed in 1847, and burnt down in 1849, was finally rebuilt as it now stands in 1850. One of the last straightforwardly classical buildings in Belfast, with its heavy Corinthian portico, it was designed by Isaac Farrell of Dublin, the leading Irish Methodist architect of his time. The exterior seems rather overgrown and lumpish, due mainly to the uncomfortably wide spacing of the columns. The interior is pleasantly conservative and rather dull, though there are good box pews and a fine pulpit.

The Assembly's College, a rather grand semi-classical-semi-renaissance stone building at the rear of the Queen's College, was opened in 1853 (Plate 25). The facade is by Charles Lanyon; despite the fine rusticated stonework, and the great Doric porch, it is rather unsatisfactory since, in lieu of a pediment, the central block terminates in a square attic storey ornamented with over-large Baroque consoles. The great library which occupies the upper floor, however, is a splendid room, divided into three by screens of Corinthian columns, with a central semi-dome. The undistinguished South wing was added in 1869; the North wing and Chapel in 1878, to plans by Lanyon's son John. The chapel is most curious, with very tall pine Corinthian pilasters around the walls, and very strange tall window-cases also of pine and also baroque in feel: one might hazard a guess that John Lanyon had recently spent a holdiay in Austria when he designed this. The library was used by the House of Commons, the chapel by the Senate, while the Parliament of Northern Ireland awaited the completion of Stormont; the resulting rent constituted a very acceptable

[37]   See W. A. Maguire, 'Lord Donegall and the sale of Belfast: a case history from the encumbered estates court' in the *Economic History Review*, November 1976.

[38]   Landed Estates Court Survey by Hodges and Smith, 1850 (copy in PRONI, ref. T 1641).

[39]   Emrys Jones, *Social Geography of Belfast*, (Oxford, 1950), p. 51.

[40]   Quoted in C. H. Brett, Notes on Topography of Old Belfast, 1870, (unpublished typescript in Linen Hall Library).

successor to the Regium Donum—a sort of Parliamentum Donum.

The seaward block and octagonal campanile of the Harbour office were completed in 1854 to the plans of George Smith, the Harbour Engineer (Plate 33).[41] The remaining parts of   * the present pile were added in 1895 by W. H. Lynn. Its original appearance was that of a merchant's villa in the Italianate style, and this air to some extent it still retains. The Board Room, which overlooked Clarendon Dock until in 1966 the latter was partly filled in to make a car-and-lorry park, is one of the handsomest rooms in Belfast, with excellent stucco panelling, heavy but simple pedimented doorcases, and good marble chimneypieces—all designed by Smith. The huge multi-columnar Public Room and the entrance hall are too consciously splendiferous to be entirely successful. Oddly, nautical motifs are entirely absent from the ornament. The building, which is shown to members of the public on request,[42] houses a quite unexpectedly rewarding collection of furniture, paintings and sculpture, for the most part presented by past members of the Harbour Board. These include 'Romney' Robinson's splendid triumphal painting of the principal inhabitants of Belfast in 1804, variously entitled 'Review of the Belfast Volunteers', 'Military Procession in Honour of Lord Nelson', and 'Entry of Lord Hardwicke into Belfast', according to taste.

Another marine building of this period is the charming small warehouse of Messrs Tedford, Ships' Chandlers, at 5 Donegall Quay, built in 1855 to the plans of Alexander McAllister (Plate 53). It is a pleasantly naïve example of nautical architecture, executed in stucco, with vertical cable-mouldings running up the crude pilasters to the gable; a lifebelt on the walls; and a large sheaf-block for a shop-sign.

Two other buildings with a strongly seaport flavour, both by Charles Lanyon, date from 1857. The Custom House is Belfast's finest public building, and the peak of Lanyon's   *** achievement (Plate 27). Built of golden stone, recently cleaned in a rather patchy and half-hearted way,[43] it is an E-shaped building 'in the Italian style, after Palladio'. The outer arms are joined by a staircase and a high plateau; the portico is a fairly plain but enormously dignified composition centred on three great round-headed windows. The building has unfortunately shifted somewhat on its foundations, perhaps not surprisingly, for it stands on the site of Daniel Mussenden's salt-pans of a hundred years earlier. The docks in High Street and Waring Street had only been filled in in 1846, at the time when Queen's Quay and the Queen's Bridge were built.

Although the monumental simplicity and the clarity of the masonry of the building as a whole are superb, its most successful feature is the seaward façade, and particularly the carving in the pediment (Plate 45). This was executed by Thomas Fitzpatrick, a really remarkable working sculptor, and consists of splendidly large and serene figures of Britannia, flanked by lion and unicorn, with Neptune and Mercury gazing out on either side through their anti-pigeon cage. Various appropriate capstans, barrels and rope-ends are introduced into the composition. The whole thing has the lazy grandeur that characterizes Victorian mason's work at its very best; not an affair of muscle, still less of bone or structure, but of mass. The interior is not equally impressive, though the Long Room is truly long. There

---

[41]   The Harbour Office itself has been well cleaned and tidied up in 1984-5; unfortunately the quality of its surroundings has degenerated due to the inappropriate modern office block next door, and the depressing wasteland of fences, railings, and parking lots.
[42]   Subject to security requirements.
[43]   Very well and thoroughly overhauled and cleaned again in 1983-4. For the changes in its appearance at different dates, see pp 36 and 37 of Brian Walker and Hugh Dixon, *In Belfast Town* (Belfast, 1984).

is a honeycomb of vaults, part stone part brick, which astoundingly accommodate a miniature rifle range for the use of the zealous excisemen.

Sinclair Seamen's Church in Corporation Square,[44] also by Lanyon and opened in the same year, is a plainish Lombardish building, with a tall square campanile, rather oddly carried out in very coarse and uneven stone; much patched with cement; pleasant in line, but over-gritty in texture (Plates 33 and 68). The church was paid for on the understanding that it should always 'be considered as specially called on to watch over the spiritual interest of seamen frequenting the port of Belfast'. Until the Reverend Samuel Cochrane, BA, RN, 'a man who, in his amiable and optimistic flight, never allowed his wings to droop',[45] was installed in 1902, it differed in no way in appearance from other Presbyterian churches, apart from its rather unusual L-shape. Mr Cochrane transformed the interior, however, into a sort of maritime museum; there is a splendid, very Moby Dick, corner pulpit, incorporating the bows, bowsprit and figurehead of the *Mizpah*, and above it the organ, bedecked with port and starboard lights, a ship's bell, and a compass rose (without a needle). There are nautical motifs everywhere: a brass Detroit ship's steering wheel and capstan: the bell of HMS *Hood*, rung before the service commences; a polished brass binnacle serving as a font, with an urn on top inscribed 'Mother': model ships on the window ledges, lighthouses on the walls, and a flying-boat, complete with illuminated wing-tip lights, cruising round the ceiling. On the walls there are brass memorial tablets shaped as sails, bells, anchors, lighthouses and lifebelts. The collection is taken up in model lifeboats, which repose in a rack in front of the pulpit when not in use.

The few sailors who go there now say there is no other church like it in the world, save one at Hamburg.

Lanyon at this period was at the peak of his career. His output was enormous; even between 1838 and 1844 he is said to have erected or helped in the design of fourteen churches in the diocese. In 1852, he built a new head office for the Northern Bank in Queen's Square,[46] a rather florid low-slung building in heavily rusticated white stone (Plate 32). As with much of Lanyon's later work, the detailing has become rather coarse, and this time the general handling of the Italian style is rather clumsy; but the customer feels no qualms as to the solidity of the establishment. In 1854, St Mark's, Ballysillan, was completed. His fame spread to Dublin, and in the succeeding years his firm built at least two churches there, and many seats for the gentry nearby; by 1861 he found it necessary to open a branch office in Dublin. At the same time, he was engaged not only on railway and engineering contracts, but also, until he resigned the post in 1860, on the duties of the County Surveyorship; and in addition found time to pour out a stream of warehouses for the Belfast linen magnates.

More and more he leaned on the services of assistants for the accomplishment of all this work. W. H. Lynn joined him as an apprentice in 1849, was taken into partnership in 1860, and remained with the firm till 1872. Thomas Drew became an apprentice in 1854, but did not remain for long; in 1862 he removed to Dublin, entered the office of the elderly and distinguished William Murray (Francis Johnston's partner and successor) and (following Lanyon's example) embarked on the high road to professional success by marrying the boss's

[44] Surviving bravely, pretty well unchanged, despite some bomb damage and a scattered congregation.
[45] *Sinclair Seamen's Church Souvenir* (Belfast, 1957).
[46] Abandoned and sold by the Northern Bank on building its new open-plan slab block in Donegall Square West; happily, bought as its computer centre by the Trustee Savings Bank; now well cared for and evidently in safe hands.

daughter. Lanyon's much less talented son John joined the firm in 1864 as a partner.[47]

With such a team around him, Lanyon took less and less personal interest in architecture. In the mid-fifties, he became active in local politics; he was elected to the Belfast Corporation, became Mayor in 1862, and from 1866 to 1868 sat at Westminster as one of the Conservative MPs for Belfast. In the latter year, however, he had the misfortune to be opposed, in the great disestablishment election, by the uncommon alliance of an orthodox Liberal, Thomas McClure, and a highly unorthodox Orange independent, William Johnston of Ballykilbeg; and after a riotous election campaign, he and his fellow-Conservative both lost their seats (Plate 28). He was at the top of his profession in this period: in 1867 he was elected President of the Royal Institute of Architects in Ireland, and in 1868 was knighted. Never, apparently, any too scrupulous in his business dealings, he began also to take an interest in property speculation during these years.

Of only two other buildings of his later years is it possible to say with fair confidence that they are the work of Lanyon himself, rather than of his colleagues. One is the exceptionally fine stone warehouse block at 9-15 Bedford Street (Plate 30). There seems to ** be no documentary evidence either for its date or for its architect; but it is clearly a first cousin of the Custom House, and appears to have been built about 1855.[48] Tall, rather thin, and very austere apart from the cornice and the round-headed windows in the fourth storey, it is admirably proportioned and all too easily overlooked in a rather strident thoroughfare. The other is the Ulster Club in Castle Place, completed in 1863.[49] Curiously, having remodelled the Belfast Bank in the style of a club-house, Lanyon chose to build the club-house in the Regency tradition. There is a heavy central bow-front, and the stucco façade is pleasantly formal, but here (as in the Northern Bank) the detailing is throughout somewhat coarse. The drawing-room on the first floor, divided into three bays by clusters of Corinthian columns, runs the full width of the house and is rather fine. There is a good cast-iron balcony.

But although Lanyon now began to rest upon his laurels, his position was by no means unchallenged. In the early fifties a remarkable young man from Newry, W. J. Barre, began to be noticed. Barre was thirteen years younger than Lanyon; he had served his apprenticeship with Thomas Duff. In 1850, before he had reached his twenty-first birthday, he set up in business on his own in Newry. Unlike Lanyon, who always remained an engineer at heart, Barre was the evangelist of ornament and of the decorated Gothic style. His Unitarian Church in Newry, completed in 1850, attracted much attention; it 'marked the commencement of an entire change in the style of architecture patronized by the Protestant Dissenting community . . . a change with which, in this country, his name is inseparably associated as the originator'.[50] In 1855 Barre secured his first commission in Belfast, for another Unitarian Church in York Street. And in the following year he came into head-on collision with Lanyon, for the first but not the last time, in lurid circumstances.

A full and, no doubt, one-sided account of the Scrabo Tower competition appears in a ✂ curious little volume, breathing white-hot indignation, published in 1868 just after Barre's

---

[47] Not all these dates are correct. Lynn became a partner in 1854; John Lanyon in 1860. See Hugh Dixon in *Irish Georgian Society Bulletin*, XVII, Jan-June 1974.

[48] In fact, 1852; see *The Builder*, 17 April 1852, pp 245-6; also Brian Walker and Hugh Dixon *In Belfast Town* (Belfast, 1984), p. 14. Alas, this excellent building was wantonly destroyed, despite the protests of conservationists, to make way for the dreadful 23-storey Windsor House office block. See also page ix.

[49] Allowed to deteriorate beyond repair after comparatively minor bomb-damage, and ultimately demolished to make way for a rather brash replacement; see also page ix.

[50] Durham Dunlop, *Life of W. J. Barre* (Belfast, 1868), p. 7.

death: *A Memoir of the Professional Life of William J. Barre, Esq;* edited by Durham Dunlop, MRIA, author of *The Philosophy of the Bath*. (It is curious that, while Barre is the only Belfast architect about whom a biography has ever been published, Lanyon is the only one to have rated an entry in the Dictionary of National Biography.) The competition was for a memorial to Lord Londonderry to be erected on Scrabo Hill above Newtownards, Co Down, and to cost no more than £2,000. Mr Barre's design—an obelisk on a pedestal—was awarded first prize; a Mr Boyd came second; drawings by Messrs Lanyon were placed third and fourth. But Lanyon got the job. It is worth quoting Dunlop at length: 'Mark the scandalous artifice resorted to—the flagrant injustice practised. While Mr Barre was tied down to have his design constructed of Scrabo frestone, *no such condition was imposed* as regards the third-rate competitor whose design was to be favoured! *He was not required to build with freestone at all!* Whinstone, rubble, surface scrapings, or anything he pleased, might be used by him, and *was* used! . . . What was to cost only £2,000, actually cost £3,010, and even then it was not properly constructed or finished, though the unfortunate contractor was ruined! With the same material, Mr Barre's design could have been built for £1,600!' [51] Victory for Lanyon; though the style of the tower, a sketch in the Scottish baronial manner, makes it look as though the designs were really Lynn's.

Nothing daunted, Barre continued to go in for competitions, which were then becoming fashionable. In 1857 he won one for a memorial in Monaghan; in the same year he lost one for the new Ulster Bank (see page 44). His indignant biographer attributed the death on 9 December 1867 of Robert Grimshaw, one of the founder-directors of the bank, and then aged eighty, to this misjudgement on the part of the adjudicators; 'one of the oldest and most respected inhabitants of Belfast, a Director of the Bank, while in the enjoyment of good health, suddenly met his death by falling down a flight of steps, which, had utility been properly consulted, he would never have been required to ascend'.[52] In 1860 Barre removed to Belfast in order to supervise the building of the Ulster Hall. Once again he had won a competition, this time in the teeth of forty-one competitors, and of 'dexterous manoeuvring' and 'artful representations' that he was too young and inexperienced to complete the job.

Even making allowance for the fact that much of the ornament was omitted on grounds of economy, it is not one of his most successful works. The exterior, of grey stucco, is rather lumpish and elephantine. It was originally crowned by a rather pleasant coat of arms supported by the old deer and wolfhound of Ulster: in 1959 the loyal burgesses of Belfast rendered themselves ridiculous by removing this and replacing it by a crude concrete red hand, from which the paint is continually peeling. The foyer was rendered equally absurd when it was repainted in Festival of Britain colours—its four enormous columns garish in bright blue: the stairs and corridors an unappetising salad of raspberry, lemon and mushroom, with more blue.

The hall itself is vast, airy and dignified, though it lacks the sparkle Barre envisaged. Corners and ceiling are alike coved—the latter also coffered, and painted blue with cream beams and red spots. There is a fine alderman-bellied balcony on pineapple-pie pillars. At the keys of the round-headed windows are twenty whiskered worthies; there are arches, pilasters, and heraldic lunettes; and below, thirteen rather pleasant, if slightly murky, scenes from Belfast history (and mythology) painted by J. W. Carey in 1903. The focal point of

[51] *Ibid.*, pp 15-16.   [52] *Ibid.*, p. 21.

the whole hall is the large pale-grey organ-case, with an oddly stove-like top.[53] Notwithstanding its peculiarities, the Ulster Hall has a very individual personality, which it imposes impartially on the boxing matches, orchestral concerts, wrestling bouts, and politico-religious rallies for which it is now mostly used; whereas it was originally designed to accommodate Balls.

During the 1860s Barre designed a number of churches; those in Belfast included the modestly charming Wesleyan Church (in a sort of red-brick Lombard Romanesque style) in University Road, and two for the Presbyterians at Belmont and Duncairn. Belmont Presbyterian Church, though so often enlarged over the years that almost nothing of Barre's original building is still visible, has acquired a very pleasing air of mellowness and antiquity, much assisted by the new (and very un-Presbyterian) square pinnacled tower added in 1900 by Vincent Craig; and by the spreading of Virginia creeper over the walls of red brick, with yellow brick dressings. The various enlargements—the south aisle and transept were added by Anthony Jackson in 1873; the north aisle by Young & Mackenzie in 1887; the church was lengthened by Vincent Craig in 1900—are congruous and harmonious, and the ultimate elaboration of the roof-timbers would have pleased Barre. He monkeyed with the ceiling of St George's; his detestation of Georgian architecture was extreme—'the architectural style of the building—that of debased Grecian—seemed to defy all attempts at improvement'. In 1862 he entered with warmth into the competition for the new cathedral of St Finbar at Cork. The conditions laid down that its total cost should not exceed £15,000; his indignation knew no bounds when the first prize was awarded to the distinguished London architect William Burges, for a design which, Barre averred, could not be executed for £30,000. 'Naturally disgusted with such conduct—indignant at the deception so shamefully practised, Mr Barre . . . endeavoured to bring the case before the Courts'; but without success. However, in the same year, he was successful in the competition for a memorial in Banbridge, Co. Down, to Captain Crozier (frozen to death while seeking the North-West passage), and erected in that town a delightfully individual composition in which four mourning polar bears rear their hindquarters in eloquent salute to a statue by Joseph Robinson Kirk of the unfortunate Crozier.

While his worst work is, it must be admitted, exceedingly funny, he was capable of better things. Much of his warehouse and factory work is gay and successful. Bryson House in Bedford Street, originally a linen warehouse, is an admirable brick building with a Venetian feeling, though its author described its style as 'Victorian, with a Gothic treatment of details'. There are four windows on the ground floor, six on the first floor, nine on the second; each has a curved hood of carved stone; the whole recession is well-proportioned and well handled. It is a pity that cleaning of the brickwork has left the building raw and pink.

Barre was ready to provide the merchants of Belfast with palatial homes as well as palatial warehouses. Indeed, he was amongst the first to cater for the luxurious tastes of the textile parvenus; tastes which seem in Belfast to have outdone the magnificence even of the English manufacturers of the Midlands. Few cities are surrounded by quite such imposing palaces as Belfast. They are now for the most part used as hotels, or institutions, or the headquarters

---

[53] More recent repainting, particularly of the organ-pipes, has been the occasion of some controversy. Next time, it might be well to seek advice, well in advance, from the most eminent authority available on Victorian décor. The Carey paintings are presently being cleaned and restored. The Ulster Hall has come into its own again as the result of the success and popularity of the Ulster Orchestra; its fine qualities, including its admirable acoustics, have been under-estimated. I should certainly today have awarded it three, not two, stars.

of commercial undertakings; but in their days of splendour they were worthy of Sir Gorgius Midas himself. Barre contributed to their number The Moat, Strandtown, and the very splendid Clanwilliam House on the Malone Road (built for Samuel Barbour; now known as Danesfort, and used as headquarters by the Electricity Board) both completed in 1864. The latter is a sort of a French-Italian-English chateau, with a highly decorated four-storey mansarded tower, bestriding the carriageway so that its foundations (square cabbagey columns) constitute a porte-cochère (Plate 35). The exterior is quite unaltered, although now surrounded by a tremendous jumble of electrical bric-à-brac. Some of the stonework is beginning to crumble; the great marble chimneypieces gaze deprecatingly down on deal canteen tables; but it is still a most princely building, and one of the most successful Barre ever built.[54]

In the same year, Barre designed the ornate gateways at either end of Fortwilliam Park, a superior residential avenue running from the Antrim Road to the Shore Road. The original gates and central pier (a strange column of pierced ironwork) have long since been removed and turned to warlike purposes; the four stone pillars, cusped and columned, survive rather pointlessly.

The former Opthalmic Hospital in Great Victoria Street, completed in 1867, is in comparison a very modest piece of work. It is an early exercise in the use of polychrome brickwork; mainly yellow, but with red bands and contrasting stone-work. Apart from the columns between the upper windows, it has no hint of the pomposity usual in a public building of this period, and could very easily be mistaken for an only slightly pretentious dwelling house.

The same could never be said of the Provincial Bank of Ireland in Castle Place. An extraordinarily exuberant building even as it stands, a great deal of the original ornament was omitted when the building was completed, after Barre's death; the pediment, bare of all decoration, would have grieved him bitterly, for he had planned an elaborate set-piece of six figures carved in high relief, surmounted by a further family group upon a pedestal. Only the seven decapitated kings on the keystones, grimly presiding over the façade, were executed. It is in a rather over-foliated Italian style; the original white Cookstown stone had to be painted in 1888 in a despairing effort to arrest its swift decay. Indeed, the architect who completed the building after his death suggested an alteration: 'They proposed to have the cold, brown-soap-coloured Scotch freestone, so suggestive of damp and discomfort,— such as the Ulster Bank is built of, substituted; . . . but happily all such arrogant profanity was prevented.[55] Inside, the very airy dome is supported on arches which, in turn, rest on squat little columns like reels of pink cotton; curious bronze-painted mannikins stand around the walls; and the internal doorways are formidable Gothic ogees, each with a carved figurehead (Plate 34). The resulting impression is surprisingly successful.

The final confrontation between Barre and Lanyon took place in 1865, and this time, despite all the odds, Barre was the victor. A competition was held for a Memorial to the late Prince Consort. Drawings were submitted anonymously; the Selection Sub-Committee

---

[54] At present undergoing a major, and most welcome, restoration, to provide accommodation for the Board, Chief Executive and secretariat of the N.I. Electricity Service. The ravages of years of neglect and decay are being made good; the unworthy surrounding nissen huts and bric-à-brac are all to be cleared away. If the work is successfully completed, Danesfort should ultimately rival the Grand Opera House and the Crown Bar as a Victorian showpiece, and be well worth every ohm, amp and volt expended in the process.

[55] Durham Dunlop, *op. cit.*, nn, (page unnumbered).

placed Barre's first, that of Messrs Lanyon Lynn & Lanyon second; but on their making a recommendation accordingly to the General Committee, the latter reversed the order. Subsequently it transpired that Lanyon (then one of the MPs for the City) was present, as a member of the General Committee, when the decision was reversed; and in consequence of the resulting scandal, the Committee shamefacedly reverted to its original choice.

Barre's design was, appropriately enough, an exercise in the German-Gothic style. It is not in the same class as the Albert Memorial in Hyde Park, but it is nevertheless a highly distinctive monument, and may come to be highly prized in time. It is now black and dingy; the crockets have been amputated from its pinnacles;[56] and it has very decided leanings out of the vertical—in 1901 it was 'noticed to have been lately considerably out of plumb'. The statue of Albert, forlorn in his Garter robes amongst the pigeons, is by S. F. Lynn, the younger brother of W. H. Lynn, Lanyon's partner; an ironic choice (Plate 42).

Although the Albert Clock constituted a final vindication for Barre in his battle with Lanyon, there were unkind whispers in 1909 to the effect that the design was really by his chief assistant, one C. Sherrie.[57] It may be so; but poor Barre died in the hour of glory. In August 1865 he had received several severe wettings while marking the site for a villa in Downpatrick in the midst of wet grass; and (like Prince Albert) 'was so imprudent as to travel without changing his clothes'. He fell ill; after a fruitless stay in Mentone, returned to Belfast, and died in the autumn of 1867.

He was a remarkable man, and one who made a very idiosyncratic contribution to the architecture of Belfast. Few of his buildings are wholly successful; he quite lacked the grasp of composition and massing that Lanyon enjoyed; yet the richness and vigour of his work projected Belfast into a new age. Though he never quite found it, all his life he was groping for the style of the High Victorian period. His affectionate biographer summed him up neatly when he said: 'While Mr Barre was exceedingly partial to the noble and inexhaustible Gothic, if he could be justly classed as belonging to any particular school it would be the *Eclectic*'.[58]

Although Barre and Lanyon were undoubtedly the dominant architects working in Belfast in the fifties and sixties, they were not quite alone. One or two outsiders were brought in. Several working builders were still capable of remarkably happy results. About this time, the 'Belfast roof' seems to have been pioneered. It was an uncommonly cheap and ingenious method (now in disrepute) of constructing a wide-span roof out of numerous short lengths of light timber. A layer of felt was placed on top of a series of segmental lattice-truss girders, built up from light scantlings. A firm named Anderson & Son built hundreds of these roofs throughout the British Isles from 1880 onwards; but a similar roof was advertised by McTear & Co in 1870, and the principle seems to go back some years earlier.

Another stream of development was represented by the Crystal Palace in the pleasure ground on the Queen's Island, long since submerged in Harland & Wolff's enormous shipyard, and the conservatories in the Botanic Gardens. The large palm-house (Plate 51), *
a fine piece of work, is clearly a descendant of Paxton's Crystal Palace of 1851, and probably only a few years later; Hitchcock records that between 1851 and 1854 New York, Belfast, Dublin, Breslau, Copenhagen and Cheltenham were all contemplating palaces of this kind.

---

[56] The stonework was well restored in 1979-80; but unhappily, no attempt was made to restore the missing crockets, clearly visible in early photographs—for example, that at page 10 of Brian Walker and Hugh Dixon, *No Mean City* (Belfast, 1983).
[57] *Irish Builder*, Jubilee Issue 1909, p. 41; article by J. Ferguson.
[58] Durham Dunlop, *op. cit.*, p. 55.

Nothing is known of the authorship of the glass-houses in Belfast.[59] Either or both might well be the work, however, of Richard Turner of Dublin (builder of the Palm Stove at Kew, and the No. 2 shed at Lime Street Station) or of his brother Thomas, an architect practising in Belfast; who obtained a 'special mention' for their unsuccessful entry in the Great Exhibition competition, which included five enormous domes crowning a super-conservatory 1,440 feet long around which the public were to travel on a miniature railway.[60]

Notwithstanding the technical developments of glass-and-iron engineering, buildings in the Georgian spirit continued to be built throughout this period. This was true not only of dwelling-houses, but also of warehouses and offices. The progression was very gradual. The block at 31-41 Franklin Street and 8-12 James Street South,[61] built about 1840, is a very fair example; now tired and grimy; sensible but uninspired. 54 Victoria Street,[62] a pleasant enough office block of stucco, painted brick-colour, with the ground floor framed in Ionic pilasters, belongs to the same tradition, and dates from about 1847. On the opposite side of the street, however, 57 to 73 Victoria Street,[63] though about contemporaneous, provide a marked contrast. Originally this extremely long demi-classical façade in now decrepit stucco must have been very effective. The ornament of the many bays is applied in an exceedingly subtle, and almost musical, rhythm. Now grossly neglected, the building is sprouting grass from the gutters and pigeons from the curious bannister-barred openings in the attic storey. But it is almost Roman in its decay; and clearly owes its inspiration to Sir James Pennethorne's development of New Oxford Street in London at the same period.

** By the 1860s, commerce had become more self-conscious. One of the most charming buildings in Belfast is 10 Donegall Square South, a delightfully naïve-sophisticated warehouse block built about 1863, and a happy meeting place of Georgian proportions and of gay and (then) novel Victorian ornament. It is built of very pleasing honey-coloured stone; but was stupidly painted cream in 1960 so as to subordinate it to its tedious modern (and much inferior) Big Brother next door. Some of the enchanting ornamental sculpture was, unforgivably, defaced at the same time.

The block has almost identical fronts to the square and to Linen Hall Street; the ground-floor windows are round-headed, the two storeys above have charming lintels of carved fruit and flowers; there is a very fine floral cornice. In the centre of each façade is a Venetian window crowned with carvings. Between the ground floor windows are lunettes with robust portrait heads, full of character, slightly larger than life: Newton, Humboldt, Jacquard, Peace, Flora, Stevenson, Tom Moore and Watt in that order face Linen Hall Street; Mlangelo, Columbus, Washington, Mercury, Minerva, Shakespeare, Schiller and Homer face the back of the City Hall (Plates 37 and 39). Both architect and sculptor are unknown.

---

59   For a full account of this building, see Eileen McCracken, *The Palm House and Botanic Garden, Belfast* (UAHS, Belfast, 1971). Dr McCracken demonstrates that the design was by Charles Lanyon, the actual construction by Richard Turner (Thomas was his son not his brother); and that the curvilinear ranges in fact antedated those both at Kew, and at Glasnevin. Admirably restored over a period of years as the City's contribution to European Architectural Heritage Year. Purists might cavil a little at the unpainted mahogany roof-lights, and the modern lamp-standards; but this structure and its later companion the Tropical Ravine (likewise very well restored) now provide the citizens with an amenity as exotic and steamy as, and more odoriferous than, a turkish bath.

60   H.-R. Hitchcock, *Early Victorian Architecture* (London, 1954), pp 533 and 549.

61   Demolished to provide part of the site of the 23-storey Windsor House.

62   Bomb-damaged; blocked up and empty; likely to be demolished soon.

63   Bombed; now the site of the small paved garden at the side of St George's church.

A diametrically different idiom is to be seen at 10-14 Victoria Street. Built in 1863 for the Scottish Amicable Life Assurance Company by Thomas Jackson, this is one of the first applications of the Bankers' Pompous style to a business headquarters. The façade is of stone, the side walls of grey brick; there is little merit about this massive and ornate elephant of a building; but it was nonetheless a significant symptom of things to come.

For the most part, however, warehouses in the 1860s were built in an uneasy compromise between the Georgian and Victorian styles. Two examples, both by the firm of Lanyon, Lynn and Lanyon, and both mainly of greyish-yellow brick, Georgian in proportion, Victorian in detail, make this clear. 16-18 Donegall Square North now houses the Linen Hall Library, but (as the linenfold drapery in the porch demonstrates) was designed as a warehouse, and completed in 1864.[64] Matier's building at 1 May Street, built in 1867, is basically similar; the red brick patterns and the Italian-Gothic window-detailing distract the eye, but on closer examination do not detract, from the basically traditional proportions.[65]

Similarly, the transition in dwelling-houses of this period, except for the very grandest sort, was very gradual. In 1859, Alex McAllister designed the tall terraces of Mount Charles. In essence, apart from the strange pierced screen wall at the rear, these constituted but a slight variant on the basic Georgian brick terrace formula. Yet these houses, 'durable and elegant', sported bay windows, 'as much the rage now as hoops and crinolines'—evidence that the Victorians were as much preoccupied by convexity as are we—and were amongst the first in Belfast to be 'fitted for hot and cold baths'.[66] In the same year, Thomas Jackson built the seven charming Jacobethan houses known as Queen's Elms, just opposite the College, demolished by the University in 1965. Both these terraces represented meeting-points between the old and the new.

Ecclesiastical architecture at this period was likewise in a stage of uneasy transition. A number of uninspired and uninspiring churches were erected by all denominations in the spreading suburbs of Belfast. A very pleasantly eccentric one is Elmwood Presbyterian **
Church in University Road,[67] built in 1862 to plans by John Corry, an amateur architect, the London director of the family firm of contractors and shipowners, and brother of the James Corry who built Upper and Lower Crescents. His other works include Dunmurry Prebyterian Church, Co. Antrim, and a remarkable Doric temple in Movilla graveyard at Newtownards, Co Down.[68] Both exterior and interior are designed on wedding-cake principles: the arcaded Italianate façade is pleasing, the three tiers of the spire are delightful. There are many small columns and curly capitals. Inside, the church is very broad for its length, and the wedding-cake impression is strengthened both by the treatment of the front of the gallery and by the coffered ceiling with icing-sugar snowflakes on a pink ground. The members of the Corry clan are very liberally commemorated throughout the building. There is a rather pretty pair of botanical stained-glass windows.

The exterior of St Peter's Roman Catholic pro-cathedral in Derby Street is impressive

---

[64] Recently overhauled externally and internally; only the protrusion of the lift-shaft from the roof strikes a discordant note.
[65] Demolished, along with the pleasant terrace of late-Georgian houses alongside, to make way for the clumsy six-storey office block which later became the Housing Centre.
[66] *Irish Builder*, 1859, p. 55. Despite damage from numerous bombs in the vicinity, still in fair order; the stucco houses fronting onto University Road had to be completely rebuilt after bombing.
[67] This church has been admirably converted by the University into a combined lecture, concert and examination hall. Much money has had to be spent on the spire, which had begun to be dangerous. The community is in debt to the University for here making amends for earlier misdeeds.
[68] J. Dewar, *History of Elmwood Church* (1900).

despite an unsuitable site. Designed by Father Jeremiah McAuley, a native of Belfast and a trained architect, who was ordained in 1858 but departed to Salamanca before the church was finished, it was completed in 1866 by John O'Neill. Its twin soaring spires (added in 1886 to plans by Mortimer Thompson) are excellent; and there is a good circular carving in the typanum of the main doorway (the angels freeing St Peter from prison). But the interior is irremediably gloomy: brown, dingy and utilitarian, with depressing mosaics, and very queasy-making woodwork, with quasi-fretwork, in the supports of the lean-to-roofed side aisles.

**   The Diocesan Offices in May Street,[69] built for the Church of Ireland in 1867, though at first glance gloomy, are òn closer inspection extremely handsome. One of Belfast's very few successful ventures in polychrome brick, the design is well-balanced and harmonious, and clearly owes something to the work of the Dublin architects Deane and Woodward at the Oxford Museum; and accordingly to Ruskin also. Though designed by Messrs Lanyon, Lynn and Lanyon, it may therefore be ascribed with fair confidence to the intellectual Gothicism of Lynn.

Early Victorian Belfast was almost entirely the work of native or at least resident architects. The two main exceptions were both banks. Sandham Symes of Dublin built the Bank of Ireland in Donegall Place in 1858. Its pure classical façade in plain dark stone was finely executed, and designed in the traditional manner; it was demolished in 1965.

***   In complete contrast is the remarkable head office of the Ulster Bank in Waring Street.[70] This was the design of a very young man, James Hamilton of Glasgow, whose competition design was preferred to that of W. J. Barre. One of the most magnificently exuberant buildings in Belfast, built of yellowish stone, it is an Italian-Romantic variation on the classical theme, and was completed in 1860 (Plates 40, 47 and 48). The designs were shown in the 1858 Architectural Exhibition in London, and the *Athenaeum* described them as 'very commendable, earnest, massive, rich and suitable'. Its site is regrettable cramped, and so narrow is Waring Street that it is hard either to enjoy it or to photograph it. The ground floor is Doric, above a high basement storey and the noble flight of steps down which the unfortunate Mr Grimshaw rolled to his death; the first floor is Corinthian; there is no true pediment, but a deep frieze surmounted by Britannia, attended by Justice and Commerce, while the rest of the roofline is crowned by twelve enormous beakers (full, presumably, of the true, the blushful Hippocrene). Drunken cherubs play amorous hide and seek in pairs amongst the arabesques of the frieze. All the carved stonework, which is exceedingly fine, is the work of Thomas Fitzpatrick.

Below, at street level, there are remarkable iron railings, elaborate as lace; and lamp standards, each sprouting a pair of wings, a pair of grinning serpents, and the heads of four greyhounds; all by Messrs Laidlaw of Glasgow. The effect at present is somewhat spoiled by the cabbage-patches in large coffins on either side of the ceremonial steps; the directors seem to have been reading Voltaire.

Inside, the domed banking-hall contains 'unsurpassable stucco' by George Crowe of

69   Abandoned by the church, in favour of very inferior (indeed unworthy) offices built under the shadow of St Anne's cathedral; adapted as a squash centre, which did not flourish; now to be converted to offices.
70   W. J. Knox, *Decades of the Ulster Bank*, (Belfast, 1965) p. 67; *Athanaeum*, January 1858. Despite intermittent damage from nearby bombs, restored and in pretty creditable order. The wine-jars on the roofline are complete, though several of their handles seem to have been blown away. No longer head office.

Belfast; mosaics; stained glass; and every inducement to linger and ponder on wealth and its advantages. Until its renovation in 1949, the building might well have served as the model for one of the Musical Banks in which Mrs Nosnibor, in Samuel Butler's *Erewhon*, worshipped: 'A magnificent building, of a strange but noble architecture . . . its venerable front adorned with all sorts of marbles and many sculptures . . . the inside . . . very lofty and divided into several parts by walls which rested upon massive pillars; the windows filled with stained glass.' [71] Despite its unworthy site and a number of unworthy modern intrusions, the Ulster Bank remains a splendid florescence of Victorian voluptuousness, and one of the precursors of the true High Victorian period that was to follow on its heels.

[71]   Samuel Butler, *Erewhon* (London, 1872), chapter XV.

FOUR

THE
HIGH VICTORIAN ERA

1867—1900

Balmoral Castle, jointly designed by Prince Albert and by William Smith of Aberdeen, was completed in 1855; Belfast Castle,[1] which was likewise intended to be a princely mansion, bears a close relationship to it. The second, and most improvident, Marquis of Donegall had died in 1844; the third Marquis, who succeeded him, had but three children: an eldest son who died in infancy: a second son, the Earl of Belfast (poet, novelist and composer), who romantically died in Naples of scarlatina at the age of twenty-five; and a daughter, Harriet, who in 1857 restored the family fortunes by marrying the eighth Earl of Shaftesbury, son and heir of the notable philanthropist.

In 1867 the Marquis wrote rather plaintively to his trustee, pointing out that Ormeau house was an ill-constructed residence; that 'his Estate was under a disadvantage for want of a more suitable Family Residence'; and seeking funds to build and furnish a new and more fitting seat for himself in the Deerpark, on the slopes of the Cave Hill overlooking Belfast and the Lough, at an estimated cost of £11,000. Payment was guaranteed by his daughter and son-in-law.[2] The plans were entrusted to Messrs Lanyon Lynn and Lanyon; the new Castle was completed in 1870, and if the ultimate cost by far exceeded the estimates, nobody seems to have complained. The Castle and the surrounding grounds were presented to the Belfast Corporation in 1934 by the ninth Lord Shaftesbury, who, unlike most of his ancestors, had spent the earlier part of his life in residence there, and even became Lord Mayor of the city in 1907.

It is a rugged and determined exercise in the fullness of the Scottish Baronial style, perched on a highly romantic site with a superb view (Plate 55). The great square tower, which closely resembles that at Balmoral, rises a full six storeys. The entrance façade, facing the steep slope of the hillside, has a deplorable porch with strapwork on its Doric columns. But the garden front is infinitely more successful. The original detailing is quite austere, apart from two great bow windows corbelled out on curving courses of botanical carving. In 1894 the principal rooms on the *piano nobile* were connected with a terrace far below by a richly serpentine outside staircase in the baroque manner. Astonishingly, this weird *tour-de-force*

---

[1] Belfast Castle is undergoing lengthy restoration after a combination of bombs, fire, and vandalism. No doubt it will be very fine when the work is completed, but one hopes the plastic downspouts, some red, some black, are only temporary.

[2] PRONI: D 2083: Letter from Lord Donegall to J. H. R. Chichester, 19 August 1867.

by an unknown architect comes off to perfection (Plate 62).

In the grounds—now engulfed in middle-class housing—there was erected at the same time a mortuary Chapel of the Resurrection in memory of the young Earl of Belfast. In this, the Countess of Shaftesbury placed a strange but magnificent life-size group in white marble of the young Earl of Belfast on his death-sofa, mourned by his sorrowing and lace-capped mother. The carving was commissioned from and executed by Patrick McDowell, RA, the Belfast-born sculptor also responsible for the 'Europe' group on the Albert Memorial.[3]

Both the chapel and the Castle bear a much closer relationship to the later work of W. H. Lynn than they do to the earlier work of Charles Lanyon, and it seems reasonable to attribute them to the former, though the senior partner is usually credited with both.[4] Indeed, though he is less honoured today, Lynn was in his way as distinguished a man as Lanyon. His temperament, however, was markedly different; whereas Lanyon was an adaptable and practical engineer, Lynn was a man of academic and intellectual tastes. He was a great competition man. In the course of his long career, Lynn won competitions, in 1858 (when he was twenty-nine) for a church in Edinburgh; in 1861 for Sydney Parliament House; in 1864 for Chester Town Hall; in 1872 for Manchester Assize Court; in 1876 for the Clark Halls, Paisley; and in 1877 for the Town Hall, Barrow-in-Furness. In 1875 he visited Quebec at the invitation of the Governor-General, Lord Dufferin, 'to advise on public improvements', and the Château St Louis there was executed to his designs. In 1910, a correspondent in the *Irish Builder* wrote that 'In the days of the Gothic Revival Lynn was a keen and brilliant student of medieval work, his ecclesiastical designs having a scholarly and refined flavour and perfect mastery of Gothic detail'.[5]

In 1872 he severed his partnership with the Lanyons; there seems little doubt that he might rightfully have taken credit for a number of buildings usually attributed to the elder Lanyon. Though in later life he turned to the Italian Renaissance style, it was as a Gothicist that he excelled. And in church architecture, throughout this period a rather prickly and uncomfortable Gothic style was *de rigueur*. The great majority of the numerous late Victorian churches of Belfast have knobbly stone exteriors, and exhibit a deliberate ruggedness which is ill-suited to the sooty air of a great industrial city.

For this was a golden age for ecclesiastical architects, if not quite so much so for ecclesiastical architecture. At a necessarily inaccurate count, Belfast (within its then boundaries) seems to have seen the erection during the sixty-three years of Queen Victoria's reign of forty-five Presbyterian churches; twenty-three Church of Ireland; eleven Methodist; and seven Roman Catholic, plus three convents and one monastery (each with its own chapel). To this staggering total of eighty-six must be added meeting-halls, mission-halls, parish halls, religious schools, rectories, presbyteries, manses, independent chapels, churches and synagogues, all but innumerable. Some were of wood, some of iron (corrugated or otherwise), very many of brick, most of stone. The aggregate sum spent on non-functional

---

[3] Pamphlet for private circulation, *The Chapel of the Resurrection*, (Belfast, 1891). Despite its respectable middle-class surroundings, this little building has been entirely wrecked by vandals: no glass remains in the windows, only the carcase still stands, there is an impromptu rubbish-tip at the very porch. Even the graves were desecrated, probably in the hope of recovering rings or jewellery. Fortunately, Patrick McDowell's marble group was removed, not before some damage had been done, and now stands in the foyer of the City Hall: very appropriately.

[4] In fact, it now seems that the designs may have been by Charles Lanyon's son John; to whom they are personally attributed in *Architect*, 25 October 1873, p. 214 and *Irish Builder*, 15 September, 1874, p. 17.

[5] *Irish Builder*, 1910, p. 640.

ornament must have run into millions. Much of it was inferior in quality; but much was very fine. There existed in Belfast a whole school of working sculptors who could turn their talents with equal vigour to carving a reredos, or a dragon newelpost for a mercantile office, or the ornamental teak and mahogany detailing for the great liners which were beginning to sail from the shipyard of Edward Harland and Gustav Wolff. On the whole it must be remarked that commerce, rather than ecclesiastical work, brought out the best in them.

In the case of the Church of Ireland, there were two great waves of building—the first mainly between 1869 and 1873, the second during the nineties. The first church of the earlier series, St Mary's, Crumlin Road, was completed in 1869 by William Slater, of London. Slater had been the partner and was the successor of R. C. Carpenter, a major figure amongst the ecclesiologists; and was mainly responsible for the completion of Lancing College after Carpenter's death. St Mary's is an attractive church; externally, it has an unusually wide semi-Romanesque spire crouching over the crossing; internally, red and white stone alternate in the pointed arches of its aisles and windows in a manner reminiscent of Vézelay, as restored by Viollet-le-duc. The roof, however, is disconcerting and unsatisfactory.

St Stephen's, Millfield (1869), St Andrew's, Hope Street (1870) and St Jude's, Ballynafeigh (1873), were all built by Thomas Drew. Born in Belfast, son of the Rector of St Anne's,[6] articled to Lanyon, and later practising in Dublin, he seems not to have been an entirely suitable person to embark on a programme of cheap churches for the working man. His was a fairly exuberant personality; he was known as a fluent and witty speaker; when invited to submit a design for a Memorial to Queen Victoria, he did so, and included proposals for re-fronting Buckingham Palace; he built himself 'a noble residence' outside Dublin, and named it 'Gort-na-Drew'; he was knighted in 1900 and died, apparently of gout, in 1910.[7] According to the *Dictionary of National Biography*, he was 'noted for a robust and virile Gothic'. It seems to have been of very uneven quality; even before its totally inappropriate refronting, St Stephen's was a fussy and cavernous church. St Andrew's,[8] on the other hand, though outside ugly and decrepit, has a tall, cool and austere interior. Its most surprising feature is the roof—from some angles like the works of a bicycle, from others like the works of a clock, a fascinating arrangement of hoops and spokes and trusses. The apse is stencilled with a leather-like pretence at a cloister in rich dark reds, greens and yellows, charming in its effect. The rather impressive (white painted) carved stone pulpit was a gift from the sculptors, the Fitzpatrick brothers. St Jude's also has some curious woodwork in its roof, but its three aisles are uncomfortably like contiguous railway tunnels.

St Thomas', Lisburn Road (1870) and Willowfield (1872), are both by John Lanyon. The former, an essay in early French Gothic, is a very large church with yellow brick interior and stone exterior, impressive in a stark kind of way. The latter has a dreadful red-brick exterior, and a rather fussy interior borne on thin quatrefoil columns. St James', Antrim Road (1871), was an ambitious church in decorated Gothic by W. H. Lynn; only the heavily buttressed spire survived the blitz of 1941.

St Matthew's, Woodvale Road,[9] is a wholly astonishing church (Plate 57). It was consecrated in 1872 to designs by Welland and Gillespie of Dublin, the architects to the Ecclesiastical Commissioners, and nobody even then seemed sure what its style was. It

---

6   In fact, Rector of Christ Church, not St Anne's.   7   *Irish Builder*, 1910, pp 168-173.
8   Demolished in 1970 for purely economic reasons, its site now a car-park.
9   The original drawings for this church are in the library of the Representative Church Body, Dublin. See Paul Larmour in *Ulster Architect*, February 1985, p. 5. I should now award this church three stars, not one.

is shaped like a trefoil; to Bishop MacNeice this appeared 'an enlarged shamrock',[10] but Lavens Ewart says that it was irreverently spoken of as 'the ace of clubs'.[11] The *Belfast News Letter*, in total bafflement, thought it must be French-Gothic, but the better view seems to be that it is Byzantine, with the addition of an Old Irish round tower (executed entirely in yellow brick). The *News Letter* is correct, however, in remarking that 'the design is perfectly unique, and unlike any other ecclesiastical edifice in the three kingdoms'.[12] The walls form semicircles, and rise to hemispherical domes; the entire weight is borne on four elliptical ribs springing from four slim Corinthian columns. The pewed interior is plastered, and painted grey except for the eastern hemisphere, which is pink. The exterior is entirely of grubby yellow brick, relieved by red bands. According to an anonymous description hanging in the porch, this extraordinary building is based on the ancient Orthodox churches of Greece and Asia Minor, and is an almost exact replica of one at Salonika. But the only trefoil church in Salonika is that of the Prophet Elias, the Eski-Serai, a domed building related to the churches of Mount Athos; and the resemblance is of the most tenuous.[13] Whatever its source, however, St Matthew's has an originality and a structural daring that make it stand out from the ruck of boring Victorian churches.

St Mark's, Dundela,[14] is one of the few buildings in Belfast designed by an English   *
architect of the first rank: it was completed in 1878 to designs by William Butterfield. Indeed, though he lived on until 1900, it is one of the last buildings he designed; his earlier fire and brashness (exemplified in Keble College, and Rugby School Chapel) seem to have been quite dissipated. The red sandstone exterior of this very large church is imposing, sited on the top of a hill dominating the shipyard gantries, and its tall square belfry is very imperious. But the interior of red and creamy stone is rather insipid, apart from details such as the single tall column supporting the arch at the west end; the curious stone loops, like pendant door-knockers, in the spandrels between the pointed arches of the nave; and the curiously-shaped finials at the bottom of the columns supporting the corbels for the roof-beams. The tile and mosaic decorations in the chancel, though original, are rather unsuccessful.

The later series is very conventional. St Barnabas', Duncairn Gardens (1893), and St John's, Malone Road (1894), were designed by Henry Seaver; St Patrick's, Ballymacarrett (1893), St Aidan's Blythe Street (1895), St Columba's, Knock (1896), and St Michael's, Shankill (1899), were all designed by S. P. Close; and All Saints', University Street (1898), by W. J. Fennell. None deserves special notice.

Of the Roman Catholic churches, St Mary's, Chapel Lane, reconsecrated in 1869, borrows a respectable antiquity from its predecessor opened with such ecumenical pomp in 1783 (see page 7). But in fact, only the side walls were retained, and the rest of the building, a simple barn-like church with a pitch-pine hammer beam roof, designed by John O'Neill, is of little distinction. It was again reconstructed in 1941, and the grotto and campanile were added in 1954: both are dreary, and waste the opportunities of an unusual site whose garden court opened up considerable possibilities.

St Patrick's church in Donegall Street, likewise on the site of a smaller and earlier chapel,

[10] J. F. MacNeice, *op. cit.*, p. 34.
[11] Lavens Ewart, *Handbook of the United Diocese*, (Belfast, 1886), p. 80.
[12] *Belfast News Letter*, 12 March 1872.
[13] See Charles Diehl, M. Le Tourneau and Henri Saladin, *Les Monuments Chrétiens de Salonique* (Paris, 1918), pp 203-11.
[14] St Mark's has been carefully restored and redecorated under the supervision of J. Dykes Bower; in excellent shape; today I should award two or even three stars, not one.

was completed in 1877 to designs by Timothy Hevey and Mortimer Thompson. Hevey was an enthusiastic young man, who had worked with the firm of Pugin and Ashlin in Dublin, and specialized in ecclesiastical work; he died at the age of thirty-three in 1878. St Patrick's is an effective and evocative Romanesque pile of crumbling red sandstone, with a tall spire, generally rather pyramidal in effect. Unfortunately it had recently to be refronted with raw pink stone, but until then had formed an exceptionally pleasing component of the Belfast landscape, largely because the soft stone had weathered so fast and so far as to make the building seem almost a natural rock-phenomenon.

Inside, it is ponderous and clumsy. The pillars and half-pillars, the latter rising to differing heights, are exceedingly uncomfortably arranged. There are strange ecclesiastical pendant strip-lights, and aerial hot water-pipes. The church contains a fine, if indistinctly visible, triptych in the Pre-Raphaelite manner by Sir John Lavery.[15]

St Joseph's, Prince's Dock Street, is a very similar church on a smaller scale. Designed by Hevey, it was completed after his death by Mortimer Thompson in 1881. The interior is disappointing; the crumbling spire, soaring above the quays, cranes, masts and warehouses of York Dock, is charming.

Another ecclesiastical building which illustrates John Piper's thesis that Victorian, like all other, architecture may have its charm much enhanced by the onset of decay is St

* Malachy's school, Oxford Street [16] (Plate 52). This tiny and delightful sample of Victorian Gothic, built in 1874 and now sandwiched between great brick slabs, is by the other leading Catholic architect of the period, Alex McAllister, who was also responsible for the Good Shepherd Convent, Ormeau Road (1869) and its original chapel (1880) which was demolished to make way for a larger chapel in 1916; for St Mary's Hall, Bank Street (1875); and for the large and, externally, forbidding St Matthew's, Ballymacarrett (1883).

The leading Methodist architects were J. J. Phillips and his son, J. St J. Phillips, who built at least eight churches in Belfast and several more in the surrounding countryside. Carlisle Memorial Methodist Church, at Carlisle Circus,[17] was completed in 1875 to designs by W. H. Lynn. It is amongst his least happy works, and though much beloved by a loyal congregation, must have a fighting claim to be Belfast's ugliest church.[18] It is executed mainly in coarse oatmealy stone, with contrasting detail in pink sandstone; this curious choice of colours lends unfortunate emphasis to an uncommonly ungraceful spire. The interior is dark and gloomy. The renovation of the outside carried out in 1966 has, on the whole, served only to emphasize the unfortunate choice of materials.

A much more interesting, if eccentric, church is Ballynafeigh Methodist, on the Ormeau

* Road (Plate 70), designed by Forman and Aston, a Londonderry firm, and completed (save for the spire, as yet unbuilt) [19] in 1899. It is, outside, a very strange adaptation of renaissance ideals to art-nouveau idioms. Above the lesser entrance door there is an extremely unusual plump tapering octagonal turret with splayed columns at the angles, and

[15]   Both the strip-lights and the hot-water pipes have now, happily, been removed and replaced by less obtrusive fitments; but the Lavery triptych is as hard to see as ever.
[16]   Restored with grant aid as a wholesale warehouse; the achievement somewhat devalued by the large and unsightly placard outside the door.
[17]   Abandoned as a place of worship; acquired for an imaginative conversion to provide an arts centre, and both studios and lodgings for young artists.
[18]   Was this uncharitable? Well, no, I stand by it.
[19]   The spire was in fact built, but soon removed, as early photographs show. The recent rendering and painting of the brick fillings have made the appearance of the building much less interesting.

brick fillings between them. Indeed, the exterior, with its many obtuse-angled protruberances and squat columns, gives no clue to the shape of the church within. The surprise is all the more delightful when it turns out that the interior is a tall and charming adaptation of the concept of an Elizabethan theatre; there is a terrific curved gallery, and a fretwork roof, both borne on high wooden columns; the whole church is light and airy in a mock-Tudor manner, and quite devoid of the oppressiveness so common in late Victorian churches.

According to the *Belfast News Letter*, it was 'architecturally an adaptation of the American-Romanesque style (!),[20] having been designed to avoid the usual cruciform plan and long nave . . . The seating has been arranged on the circular system, the pulpit forming the centre, so that every person has a comfortable and uninterrupted view of the speaker'.[21] This unusual plan springs from Alfred Forman's interest in acoustics; and in this respect the church is entirely successful. It was sympathetically restored and repainted in 1966.

Presbyterianism, which in earlier years had ornamented Ulster with many of its most pleasing churches, was at a low ebb architecturally at the close of the nineteenth century. The sturdy and puritannical Scottish settlers originally built plain and unadorned preaching-houses. Gradually these barn-churches came to be adorned with the paraphernalia of classicism—columns, pilasters, and pediments. The Ionic church of 1829 in May Street, the Doric Church of 1833 formerly in Rosemary Street, represented the highest point of this admirable tradition. But in the mid-century, antipathy to the 'Georgian' and the classical mounted; and a corresponding pressure arose in favour of the Gothic style for every kind of ecclesiastical building. It was to this pressure that W. J. Barre gave such forceful expression. In the end, even the most puritan of Presbyterians had to give way, though not without grumbling. The Presbyterian community, however, had no earlier Gothic tradition to look back to; the carving, the decoration, the gargoyles and traceries of high Gothic were repugnant to the austere followers of Calvin and Knox. It follows that Presbyterian Gothic lacks conviction; and the very numerous Presbyterian churches of Belfast accordingly display an almost universal mediocrity.

A good example of the dilemma facing the old-fashioned Presbyterian may be seen in Townsend Street.[22] This is a remarkable mongrel of a church. The façade and cathedral-Gothic doorway facing Melbourne Street are fine. The side view is less impressive, largely because of the clumsy way in which the buttresses protrude through the roofline. The tower (added later) rather aspires to be a spire, but funks it at the last minute. Inside, the battle of the styles rages. Intrinsically, this is a very tall and broad Georgian preaching-house, with a curved rear wall and seating arrangements like those of a continental parliament. The columns on which the gallery is borne are demi-Corinthian; but four on each side are carried on up—and another excruciatingly threaded through the gallery—to culminate in round arches. The windows are timidly cusped; and the organ has been crammed in front of a part-classical part-Gothical false window.

Townsend Street Church was completed in 1878 by the firm of Young and Mackenzie, who very rapidly established themselves as the leading Presbyterian church architects, as indeed they remain to this day. The firm built at least twelve Presbyterian churchs in Belfast in the last twenty years of the century, none of any distinction. Robert Young had been born

[20] 'That okapi amongst architectural modes'—as Osbert Lancaster remarked in another, but not dissimilar, context.
[21] *Belfast News Letter*, 13 January 1899.
[22] Now uncomfortably cut off by the canyon of the westlink road.

in 1822 at Whiteabbey; apprenticed to Charles Lanyon, and his principal assistant on the Ballymena railway; he then spent several years as engineer to William Dargan, the notable railway and canal contractor. Eventually he became a Privy Councillor for Ireland, retired from practice in 1909, and died in 1917.[23] He was followed by his only son, an antiquarian and local historian of some note, who was born in 1851 and died in 1925, having been responsible for most of the firm's church work since the 1880s.

Some Presbyterian churches were built without architects: the rather impressive Fortwilliam Church, Antrim Road, was built by an engineer named Henry Chappell. It must be acknowledged, however, that the distinction between architects and engineers was not clearly defined before the end of the century. One other church deserves a mention: the Crescent Presbyterian Church [24] in University Road, which takes advantage of a splendid site on the slopes of the Malone ridge to rear to the skyline an unorthodox but very pleasing campanile, comprising a neat little four-square roof perched on eight tall, slender and widely-spaced square columns. The church is sited with some subtlety at an angle to the road, so that the light strikes through the interstices between the verticals. This church, completed in 1887, is the work of a Glasgow architect, John Bennie Wilson, author of six churches in that city.

If the High Victorian period was a depressing one for church architecture, it saw a superb florescence of commercial architecture. To the Georgians, a shop or an office building was simply a dwelling house whose ground floor was used by the occupant to earn his living. Indeed, even the impressive shops built towards the end of the nineteenth century often contained living accommodation upstairs. There was at first no very clear distinction between an office, a counting-house, a warehouse, and a shop. But by degrees a definite commercial architecture emerged; and the trend towards ostentation, originally set by the banks, gathered momentum.

The insurance companies were the first to follow the example of the bankers; by the middle of the century the merchants and middlemen, and in the last quarter of the century even the shop-keepers, got caught in the rat-race. Du Maurier's Sir Gorgius Midas, who displayed £20,000 worth of plate on his dinner table, certainly invested a similar sum in marble and mahogany for his office; the Belfast parvenus followed suit.

This trend towards the ever-more-ostentatious, which continued down to 1914 despite a growing current of reaction, had two very disparate consequences.

On the one hand, it led to an uncertainty in taste. Georgian building at its best is austere, at its worst exceedingly dull; but it is always governed by a rigid canon of conventions. The High Victorians threw all the conventions overboard; in consequence, errors of taste were potentially more disastrous than at any other period. At its worst, High Victorian commercial can be as bad as the gross vulgarities which marred the Elizabethan period in England; but at its best it can be as good as the equally ornate styles of, say, William Kent or the Grand Siècle.

On the other hand, the desire for an air of stability brought with it an increase in real stability. The nineteenth century saw first a gradual decline from good brickwork to sleazy

[23]   *Irish Builder*, 1907, p. 793.
[24]   Acquired from the Presbyterian congregation by the Plymouth Brethren when the latter emigrated from the lamented Victoria Music Hall (see page 27). Unfortunately, the Brethren insisted on destroying the agreeable carved stone inscription, AXPIS 'OS AV EΛθN, over the main door—an appropriate fragment of classicism for University Road!

stucco. But in the fifties standards began to improve: stone came more and more into use, often imported over large distances; where brick was used, it was often fancy brick, but usually well-laid. By the end of the century, concrete frameworks were not uncommon. The blitz proved the point when many solid commercial structures of the High Victorian period survived their earlier and (for that matter) their later neighbours. Though standards of taste were variable, standards of workmanship have never been higher.

Belfast is [25] exceptionally rich in examples. Amongst the finest is the double block at 34 and 36 Victoria Street, completed in 1868 to designs by William Hastings (Plates 36, 38 and 44). Both these semi-detached warehouses were built for, and are still occupied by, firms of seed merchants, John Lytle and Samuel McCausland, then (but no longer) competitors.[26] They are ornate four-storey twins with slightly differing characters, but both in a rich Renaissance style. The chief glory of each lies in the superb carving carried out by Thomas Fitzpatrick, from detail drawings by one James Kendall. Each has a profusion of differing ornamented keystones. No. 34 is the less ornate, but has very good heavy iron window-frames, and its side elevation in Marlborough Street has a splendid helmeted Chinaman, with long drooping moustaches and pigtail, and a blubber-lipped Negro, in the keystones to its arched gateways.[27] The ground-floor façade of No. 36 is divided into bays by five half-caryatid pilasters, symbolizing the five continents and their fruits in a mouth-wateringly juicy manner. The vigour of the carving is tremendous. Both buildings have swashbuckling parapets pierced in patterns of curlicues; in both the admirable detailing is well subordinated to the elaborate rhythms and recessions of the façade as a whole.

Another vigorous piece of sculpture of this period was lost on the demolition of the Scottish Widows' Fund offices at 2 High Street in 1961. This rather severe and Caledonian building in the Renaissance style had been erected by the firm of Boyd and Batt in 1869, and was surmounted by a charming roof-top group portraying the inconsolable Scottish widow and her fatherless bairns being consoled by a stream of sooty goodies distributed by a lady with a cornucopia.

In the same year, W. H. Lynn built what was perhaps his most successful achievement, and certainly his most successful venture into the realms of commerce. This was an enormous warehouse at 1 Donegall Square North, built for Messrs Richardson Sons and Owden, linen merchants (Plate 56). It is now used as the headquarters of the Belfast Water Commissioners, who bought it just before the war; internally it was completely gutted in the blitz, and its original tall roof has disappeared.[28] Notwithstanding this, it is still one of the best buildings in Belfast, a massive merchant's palazzo in rich brown stone. The façade is in the Ruskin-Venetian manner, the cornice heavily consoled but otherwise unornamented; indeed, apart from the central balcony and the arrangement of arcaded windows and pillars above it, and the plain shield and lozenge medallions let into the wall between the windows, there is very

**

***

[25] Not is; was.
[26] Sold in favour of more convenient and accessible premises, and bought by Roads Service for demolition (!) in 1975; after protests, reprieved by Historic Buildings branch for preservation; but despite many to-ings and fro-ings over nearly a decade, no new use has yet been found. This is a lamentable saga. Three stars, I think today.
[27] The Chinaman lives on, but the Negro has gone; his nose got broken in the fight; he was rescued by Historic Monuments and Buildings Branch.
[28] Admirably restored at vast expense by Marks & Spencer Ltd, a long job finally completed in 1985. The tall roof, but not the tall dormers and chimneys, replaced; this, contrary to some fears, has been an entire success. The architects, Scott Tallon & Walker, have displayed exceptionally sensitive attention to even the smallest details: much stonework and ironwork had to be replaced.

little ornament, and the frowning grandeur of the design is allowed to speak for itself. Originally, a very tall roof in the French château style was crammed on top of the Italianate façade; the roofline is now distressing, but perhaps not much less incongruous. When Oscar Wilde lectured in Belfast on 'the House Beautiful' on New Year's Day, 1884, he was reported as saying that 'In Belfast they had, at any rate, one beautiful building. He referred to the Edifice of the Messrs Richardson Sons and Owden which was beautiful in colour, and very beautiful in design'.[29]

*   The robust and handsome Ulster Brewery in Sandy Row,[30] designed by Alex McAllister, also dates from 1869. The very satisfying pediment carving looks as though it might well be from the hand of Thomas Fitzpatrick (Plate 41). Plough Buildings in Cornmarket,[31] a pleasant stone building now occupied by Boots', dates from the same vintage year, and is by Thomas Jackson and Son. The nearby Masonic Hall in Arthur Square, also completed in 1869, is attributed to Sir Charles Lanyon (himself a panjandrum in the Masons), and if so must be almost his last work; its exterior, Gothic and frilly with a dog-tooth string-course, is grey-painted and discouraging.

Sir Charles' son John carried on the firm with declining success until his death at Teneriffe in 1900. Much of his time was devoted to railway work. His style may conveniently be compared with his father's at the South-East corner of Donegall Square; Matier's building (see page 43) is by the father; 1-3 Donegall Square South by the son.[32] Completed in 1874, it demonstrates the comparative clumsiness of the younger man. The strategem by which the tall pilasters in the red stone façade turn out to be the chimneys is disconcerting: the corner turret with lancet windows is incongruous. Even less successful are his towering red-brick Gas Offices in Ormeau Avenue,[33] built in 1893, very fortress-like, with angled towers at the ends of the mass and, again, diagonally placed lancet windows. Perhaps John Lanyon's most successful work is the Northern Bank [34] in Royal Avenue, opened in 1885; its demi-Palladian façade of honey-coloured stone is relieved by enormous columns and pilasters of rich plummy polished marble. There are two charming projecting attic loggias, surmounted with urns, but the central feature in which the chimneys are incorporated is unsatisfactory. Evidently John Lanyon found chimneys as bothersome as most contemporary architects find water-tanks and lift-shafts.

The Lanyons were not the only father-and-son partnership practising in Belfast. In two other cases it is now impossible to distinguish with certainty between the work of members of the same family: the Jacksons, and the Batts.

Thomas Jackson senior, who had built the Old Museum in 1831 and St Malachy's Church in 1844, was born in Waterford in 1807 and lived on until 1890. His son Anthony T. Jackson carried on the practice until 1908.[35] Both he and his father seem to have been very uneven

---

29   *Northern Whig*, 3 January 1888.
30   Demolished, despite strong local feeling in favour of the retention of at least 'the Brewery Arch'. A few battered fragments retained as a sop, and built into the new glass-house style community centre, where they do not look at home. The best part, the pediment and its carved tympanum, dismantled but sadly damaged in the process.
31   Demolished and redeveloped.
32   Both demolished and insensitively redeveloped: for Matier's building and its replacement the Housing Centre, see page 43: as for 1-3 Donegall Square South, this was demolished and replaced in 1969 by an ugly office block cladded in pink concrete panels, already happily beginning to crumble.
33   Bombed, burned out, and demolished.
34   Well restored after minor bomb damage.
35   Private information from family sources. See also Hugh Dixon, *Proceedings of BNHPS*, Vol 9, 1978, p. 28.

pertormers. Their practice was a varied one. In 1871, they designed the red-brick Town Hall (Plate 54) in Victoria Street (superseded in 1906 by the City Hall, and since put to a wide variety of municipal and other uses). The original drawings were too modest; 'The public offices in Belfast, when first designed, were without a parapet; the townspeople protested that it was not a public building, not having a parapet; and so great was the agitation that the plans had to be submitted to the Treasury for consideration'.[36] Present-day ratepayers are unlikely to emulate this admirable insistence on adornment.

Much more successful was the Hospital for Sick Children in Queen Street, opened in 1878, and now used as a police station.[37] It is a distinguished stone building in a dignified Scottish Renaissance style. Public buildings apart, the Jacksons were responsible for St Enoch's Presbyterian Church, Carlisle Circus, in 1872; for several merchants' villas in the suburbs, including Glenmachan,[38] Glenmachan Tower (now a hotel) and Altona; for a splendid new gutta-percha shop at the corner of Lombard Street [39] (No. 24) in 1878; for the curious asymmetrical triple block at 39-43 High Street, incorporating the Central Hall, and also Belfast's first specially designed photographic studio;[40] and for Forster Green's block at 103-105 Royal Avenue. This is rather a fine four-storey block on a curved corner site, originally with an Ionic order subdividing the plate-glass on the ground floor, pilasters running to the third floor, and a rather original (if somewhat unhappy) arrangement of triple windows on the first floor, the central window only being enclosed in a pedimented aedicule.

Less is known about the Batts. At the beginning of the century a noted Belfast divine had rejoiced in the name of the Reverend Narcissus Batt. One Robert Batt is credited with the design of Stranmillis House about 1855. The firm of Boyd and Batt practised in the 1860s; but George Boyd abandoned private practice and became building surveyor to the municipality. The most notable member of the firm is mentioned as William Batt *junior* in 1872,[41] and conducted a vigorous practice in the High Victorian style until his death in 1910.

In his earlier years, he built many plump and prosperous villas for the upper-middle classes on the Malone Road; and was for several years preoccupied with the design of the charming small gatelodge at the entrance to the Botanic Gardens (wantonly demolished in 1965). On this he lavished much loving care; the first plans were drawn up in 1876; but three years later he abandoned them, and the lodge as built was in the Venetian Gothic style, all the carved motifs being botanical, 'carved by Mr Alex. Steven and most creditable to him'.[42] Later he undertook a measure of church work, and built several Orange Halls: that in Ormeau Road, completed in 1887, he prudently fitted with 'two of Boyd's patent foul air extractors'.[43] Two years later he completed the much larger Belfast Orange Hall at 82 Clifton Street. This excellent stone building was originally very plain, discreet and unassuming; the only hint of its purpose was a single modest orange lily carved on the

---

[36] *Irish Builder*, 1873, p. 56. Very well restored to provide a new Recorder's court and ancillary offices in 1983; will look very handsome once again if ever the protective security screens can be taken down. Stop press: very severely bomb-damaged, July 1985.
[37] Now devalued by its (very necessary) surrounding security screens and guard-house; but intrinsically still intact.
[38] Unhappily vandalised and now going, going, gone; about the last of the old linen merchants' palaces.
[39] Still standing, but the ground floor spoiled.
[40] A little mutilated, but not too much; though the studio lights have gone.
[41] *Irish Builder*, 1872, p. 133.   [42] *Ibid.*, 1879, p. 100.   [43] *Ibid.*, 1887, p. 296.

keystone of the central arch. However, on its completion it was surmounted by an equestrian statue (the only one in Belfast) of King Billy, cantering south-eastward down Clifton Street and waving his sword not towards the Boyne, but in the general direction of Liverpool.[44] The statue is of bronze, ten feet high, weighs thirty-seven hundredweights, and the 'stirrups, saddlecloth and pistol holster were cast from the originals in the possession of the Baroness von Steiglitz'.[45] The statue is by Harry Hems, of Exeter, a remarkable figure whose name will recur.

**   William Batt was also responsible for the block which is now Blair's at 5-19 Church Lane. This interesting façade is still exactly as it was in 1879, and is accordingly both rare and valuable.[46] It comprises a repetitive pattern of sixteen round-headed windows, arcaded on cabbagey capitalled pilasters, showing how floribundity had become necessary even to shopkeepers. There are good cast-iron window-frames. Indeed, this building demonstrates how the practical demands of light in shop and office windows could be met despite a substantial measure of ostentation.

**   The highest peak of William Batt's career, and indeed the highest peak of High Victorianism in Belfast, is the office of the National Bank in High Street, completed in 1897. It is an exceptionally fine, grubby, and ugly building; and has recently been rendered ridiculous by the unforgivable refacing of the ground floor in wildly inappropriate black marble in the contemporary manner.[47] Of the building's exceptional strength there can be no doubt: the whole of the front wall, floors, chimneys and roof are of concrete: the architect boasted of it at the time, the blitz proved his point when the bank reared its five proud storeys above a sea of debris. Externally, it is a strange composition of brick and (now dingy) terra-cotta, the last 'of very enriched composition', modelled by the makers at Ruabon, North Wales, from special designs by the architect. The front terminates in two pinnacled pavilions. Inside, Batt was particularly proud of the patent undrillable, unbreakable, compound-steel burglar-proof treasury, the door electrically operated by a night bolt in the manager's bedroom.[48] (But why? 'Darling, I hear a burglar: open the safe so that he won't come up here'?)

The firm of Young and Mackenzie, though in its earlier years its practice was almost exclusively ecclesiastical, gradually widened its scope. In 1878 it built the warehouse block at 15 Donegall Square West,[49] originally a lacy and very handsome example of Ruskin-Venetian at its best, the skyline seen against the hills a delight. Unhappily, it was shorn in 1960 of its pinnacles, and of all ornament save the rather vapid doorway; and coated in a nasty rendering. In 1880 the firm built the forbidding and unfriendly mass of the Belfast Royal Academy, Cliftonville Road; its stark stonework must have struck awe into the hearts of generations of schoolboys-to-be.

Their break-through into the commercial field came with the commission to build Robinson & Cleaver's enormous department store at the corner of Donegall Place and Donegall Square North.[50] This remains one of the most prominent and distinctive features

44   His sword was blown out of King Billy's hand by a bomb, which left him otherwise unscathed, it has now been replaced, but not quite at the right angle.

45   *Irish Builder*, 1889, p. 280.

46   Demolished; now the site of a multi-storey car-park.

47·   The upper storeys conscientiously restored, 1984; but no attempt made to set the ground floor to rights again. I no longer think this building 'ugly'.

48   *Irish Builder*, 1897, pp 24-7.

49   Demolished by the Northern Bank to provide part of the site for its new headquarters.

50   Closed down as a department store, 1984; acquired for refurbishment as shops and offices. The grand staircase removed, the interior undergoing much alteration: the exterior stonework being cleaned and renovated at the time of writing.

of the city centre with its three phallic domes; it is sad that its bulk, silhouette and proportions should be so uniformly depressing. Its six stone storeys are not, in fact, overornate; the variations on a sub-classical Venetian window theme are by no means unpleasing; much of the detail is intriguing. This ambitious building aroused much public interest at the time: the *Irish Builder* remarked dubiously on its completion, 'The style selected is undoubtedly what may be defined as Victorian'.[51] The builders boasted that its materials included 30,000 cubic feet of sandstone, 6,000 cubic feet of concrete, 4,300 square feet of polished Aberdeen granite, 25½ miles of electric wire, 30,000 square feet of polished teak and mahogany, and about 3,000 square feet of mirrors.

As if this were not enough, 'each front of the building in enriched by elaborate carving emblematic of the business relations of the firm with all the countries of the world . . . of the Queen's Jubilee . . . and some of the most distinguished of Messrs Robinson and Cleaver's customers.' Those identifiable with field-glasses include: the Queen (of course); the Emperor and Empress of Germany; the Maharajah of Cooch Behar; Lady Dufferin, 'in appropriate costume'; and General Washington.[52]

All these were carved by Mr Harry Hems, of Exeter. This extraordinary man, as well as being an accomplished craftsman, had a gift for publicity and self-advertisement. In 1909 he mentioned modestly (in a letter to the press), 'I happen to possess over 35,000 press notices of myself all bound up and indexed'.[53] Born in Islington in 1842, he worked in his youth as a journeyman in Belfast, Dublin and Italy. Every year he held a well-advertised dinner-party for his English, Irish, Scotch, Welsh, German, French and Italian workmen to commemorate the anniverary of his finding of Ye Luckie Horseshoe. He exported carvings all over the world; in 1895 he even succeeded in portraying in stone 'a voluptuous *fair-haired* woman, draped scantily, principally about her feet', symbolizing 'Life', for an Insurance Office in Calcutta.[54]

This, of course, was a golden age for working sculptors. There are surprisingly few free-standing statues in the city. The bronze statue of the young Earl of Belfast (see page 38) by Patrick McDowell, erected by public subscription in 1855, was first placed in College Square. For some unfathomable reason, the bronze was painted black (the blacking has now worn thin; the Earl's shoes appear to need polishing): in consequence, it soon became universally known as 'the Black Man'. In 1876 the original statue was removed; it rested for some years in the Public Library, and now stands at the head of the stair-well under the dome of the City Hall. Lord Belfast was replaced on his original plinth by a statue of Dr Cooke, the noted Presbyterian divine, who still stands in College Square. Though the Doctor is in fact green, the old nickname has stuck to the site, and he is still referred to as 'the Black Man'. In view of his turbulent career, this is not wholly inappropriate; for Cooke was largely instrumental in weaning the Presbyterians of Ulster away from their old alliance with the Liberals and Catholics against the Establishment, and substituting a new alliance with the Unionist Episcopalians against the Catholics. He is depicted in clerical and academic dress. The statue, by S. F. Lynn, is said to be a very striking likeness; it was inaugurated on 24 April 1876 by a great demonstration of Orangemen from all parts of Ireland.

A fellow-cleric, the Rev. Hugh Hanna, founder of St Enoch's Presbyterian Church, stands

---

[51] *Irish Builaer*, 1888, pp 68-9.
[52] Leaflet, *Robinson & Cleavers*, Marshall Scrapbook IV, Linen Hall Library, Belfast.
[53] Obituary, *Devonian Year Book* for 1917, pp 65-6.   [54] *Irish Builder*, 1895, p. 167.

in the centre of Carlisle Circus,[55] unveiled in 1894, he is the work of Mr C. B. Birch of London. The delightful life-size portrait of Queen Victoria wrapped in Nottingham lace in the wall of the Durham Street Primary School [56] (Plate 43) is by an unknown craftsman; the school was built in 1896 to designs by S. P. Close. Statues apart, there are great numbers of carved architectural details which prove uncommonly rewarding. There are very many admirable keystones over arches, doorways and windows, some with portrait heads, some with intricate floral designs. The offices of the *Belfast News Letter* at 59 Donegall Street (a château-type structure built by William Hastings in 1873) display eight literary portrait heads in lunettes. On the opposite side of the street, No. 10 [57] actually employs the wreathed heads of mythological figures in lieu of capitals at the top of the columns framing a three-light window. Sculpture was to be found in factories too; the Mulhouse Works (in Mulhouse Street) has a series of excellent keystones, and its roofline used to be crowned by a row of noble ladies known as 'the Mulhouse virgins'—they were removed, however, from considerations of safety, at the start of the Second World War.[58] Statuary even sometimes spread to private houses, as in the curious terrace at 19-25 Inverary Drive,[59] opposite Sydenham station. There are charming gilt jumbos between the boxes in the Grand Opera House, built in 1895.[60]

There are also various curious small monuments, such as the Thompson Memorial Fountain of 1885, outside the BBC; built of crusty red sandstone like the dregs of the port bottle, it is inscribed with the text 'Who so drinketh of the water that I shall give him . . .' but has run dry; it is a sitting target for facetious graffiti, in which Belfast has always been so rich. There is also the pleasant, ornate little Calder Memorial Fountain in Albert Square, in memory of Commander Calder, RN, who between 1843 and 1855 caused ten water troughs to be erected for the use of cattle in Belfast—'A righteous man regardeth the life of his beast'.

   *   Another remarkable ornament to the city is the tremendous fountain (now likewise run dry) in the centre of the tiny Dunville Park,[61] on the Falls Road (Plate 61). There is an enormous outer dish, incorporating a kind of tombstone with an inscription with ducks on it; the central feature of stone and ornate terra-cotta comprises a bowl held up on eight columns, surmounted by four ladies with sprouting beakers on their heads; but the beakers of these foolish virgins have run dry too. The whole composition makes a splendid adventure playground for the children of the surrounding streets.

There is much excellent cast-iron work to be seen, though it is being torn down at a great rate.[62] The delightful Parisian lavatory in Victoria Square (Plate 50) erected about 1894 by

55   No longer: an early victim of the bombing, he was blown off his legs; and only his inscribed plinth remains, looking rather foolish.

56   The school demolished: Queen Victoria saved in the nick of time, and now in the care of the National Trust, awaiting a suitable time and place for re-erection. The statue was found to be inscribed on the back 'John Cassidy Fecit 1897'. John Cassidy, born in 1861 in Slane, worked as a barman in Drogheda, attended Manchester Art School, and seems to have spent most of his working life there.

57   Demolished.   58   They seem mysteriously to have utterly disappeared.   59   Gone.

60   Here I must acknowledge my failure sooner to appreciate the merits of the Grand Opera House—now beautifully restored by the Arts Council, the jumbos once again in tip-top form; today I should certainly accord the building three stars. See *Country Life*, 27 November 1980; and *Frank Matcham, Theatre Architect* (Belfast, 1980), edited by Brian Walker.

61   Now very seedy and run-down, but nevertheless an invaluable playground for the children of the Falls Road.

62   There is not much left now.

MacFarlane's of Glasgow, was demolished in 1966, but happily is to be re-erected elsewhere by the National Trust.[63] There are several pretty bandstands and fountains in the public parks. Most of the lamp-posts and other street furnishings of this period, however, have disappeared. All the other ornamental trades flourished: the pubs of Belfast still retain many beautifully engraved ornamental mirrors. There are also some very fine engraved glass windows,[64] notably those of the Boyne Bridge Tavern, Sandy Row, with a primitive but charming picture of Sir John McNeill's original lattice bridge at Drogheda; and those of the Great Eastern Bar in the Newtownards Road. A number of pubs, including Lavery's in Bradbury Place, still sport glass doors emblazoned with the title, 'Gin Palace'. There are stained-glass doors in the Pre-Raphaelite manner in the 'Windsor Castle', Dublin Road.

Indeed, one the finest High Victorian buildings in Belfast is a pub: the Crown Liquor   ***
Saloon in Great Victoria Street [65] (Plate 59). Its exterior is pleasantly gaudy; the ground floor is a riot of colourful tiles or painted glass. The upper part of the façade is ornamented with four cheerfully truncated pilasters. But the interior is of almost unbelievable richness. The ceiling is a swirling pattern of red and yellow arabesques in high relief; it is supported by hexagonal wooden columns with Corinthian capitals and feather ornament, each feather picked out in gilt. The marble surface of the bar is divided at intervals by oak screens of arches and classical columns, the bar itself being faced with gaily-patterned tiles. Behind the bar, a series of arched and pillared recesses house casks with splendid brass pipes and taps; above the arches and in the spandrels are glittering patterns and lettering on mirror-glass. The windows are painted with curling designs in blue, yellow and green; the sunlight filtered through them falls on a series of panelled snugs, their doorways surmounted by rows of heraldic lions and griffons, bearing in their paws shields inscribed alternately 'Verus Amor Patriae' and 'Audaces Fortuna Juvat'.

Though there are one or two *art nouveau* touches, and though strip lights and chromium stools constitute something of an intrusion, the Crown remains an almost entirely unspoilt example of the very richest and most mellow period of pub architecture. It seems to date from about 1885; it is said that the original pub on the site, known as the Railway Tavern, was bought by one Michael Flanagan, whose son was a student of architecture who travelled to Spain and Italy; and that the latter was responsible for its present appearance.[66]

Belfast is rich in pubs, but there are no other interiors equal to that of the Crown; nor, indeed, have I seen its equal in any other city in the British Isles. The Beehive [67] pub at 193 Falls Road, built in 1888, has a very fine stucco façade, with a most convincing beehive (and bees) incorporated in it (Plate 58); part of its ground-floor has recently been inappropriately refronted. The Morning Star, in Pottinger's Entry off High Street, has an

[63]   Still in the care of the National Trust, awaiting the right time and place for re-erection.
[64]   Glass windows, whether stained or engraved, are the very first casualties of bomb or riot: all those mentioned in this paragraph have been destroyed in one or other such episode. The Great Eastern is now the Ulster Arms; the Windsor Castle is bombed, bricked up, and derelict.
[65]   After a fair amount of damage, especially to the painted-glass windows, the Crown was acquired in 1978 by the National Trust, which, in partnership with Bass (Ireland) Ltd, has undertaken a laborious, expensive and highly successful restoration. The original gas lamps are once again both in working order, and in use; the strip lighting has been removed; the furnishings are now once again seemly and appropriate. There is still some work to be done, and repeated outbreaks of dry rot have caused problems.
[66]   Jack Loudan, undated leaflet, *The Crown Bar*.
[67]   The Beehive was severely bomb-damaged, and its façade has yet to be properly restored; but the Beehive itself survives. Designed by J. J. McDonnell: *The Architect*, Vol. 39, 27 January 1888, p. 2.

unusual wrought-iron-and-glass pub sign sprouting from a winged lion of St Mark at the corner of the building (Plate 46). Other unusual signs include a magnum of stout, five feet high, in Frederick Street; and a very solid elephant in Upper North Street.[68]

An interior almost as magnificent as that of any pub, and in a somewhat similar style, is to be found unexpectedly in the offices of the Belfast Gasworks at 2-18 Ormeau Road. In fact the Gasworks, on a site covering 27 acres, still constitutes something of an architectural treasure house; it is shortly to be demolished, however, and the process of dismantling has already started.[69] Almost nothing remains of the original buildings (see page 18) save an inscribed stone commemorating its foundation by the Marquis of Donegall in 1821.

At one end of the range of towering brick is Klondyke House, an enormous, tall, wide echoing Piranesian store, with all the evocative gloom of an abandoned cathedral, dating from 1891 (though the Bonanza at the Klondyke was not until 1895). Its end, facing the Ormeau Road, might easily have been an enormous boring brick gable; but it is skilfully relieved by brick panelling and by a terra-cotta frieze, and rises to a tremendous brick pediment incorporating a vigorous stone carving of the coat of arms of Belfast. At the other end of the range stands the office block, with its round clock tower. The erratic *genius loci* was one James Stelfox, General Manager and also Engineer to the concern, who combined a deep love for classical architecture with a technical talent for up-to-date methods and materials. Born in Salford in 1842, he removed to Belfast when his father was appointed Gasworks Manager in 1852; and succeeded him in the post in 1875. He built, about 1880, the Middle Section Meter House: an elegant pink pleasure-dome, with extensive classical panelling, a handsome plaster frieze, and a coved wooden ceiling supporting a great dome of iron and painted glass—the latter mostly, alas, destroyed in the blitz. Inside were two great cast-iron meter-houses; two more were left out in the wet. The meter-houses themselves were remarkable objects, constructed in every particular on the lines of classical mausolea, complete with pediments, pilasters and anthemia: save that, where the epitaphs should have been, were dials with whirling needles.

His triumph, however, was the office block, dating from 1888 (Plate 60). The entrance hall and staircase form an astonishing composition. They are in strict, if clumsy, classical idiom; but Corinthian pilasters, pedimented doorcases, even the fat balusters of the balustrade, all are executed in gleaming tiles—plain chocolate, milk chocolate, and a yellowish khaki in colour. Though there are some handsome interiors inside the innumerable mills and factories built in the city during the late nineteenth century, I know of no other so sumptuous.

[68]   The Morning Star's wine-jug, like those on top of the Ulster Bank, has lost one of its handles in the Troubles; the magnum of stout in Frederick Street has been finally consumed; and the poor elephant in North Street is beginning to show symptoms of disintegration: no longer a pub, now a wine shop, the top storey open to wind and weather.

[69]   This statement was premature when written, though it appears likely all too soon to come true. Coal gas production ceased in 1978, since when it has been piped five miles from Sydenham into the gas-holders at Ormeau Road. It has now been decided to close down the entire system. In these circumstances, it is no wonder most of the buildings on this 27 acre site are seedy and vandalised. Only the splendid hall and staircase remain intact. The middle section meter-house is a tragic wreck. The roof of Klondyke House is caving in, it is no longer used or usable even for storage; the army look-out post under the eaves is now abandoned. In 1969, a bomb laid beside the most capacious (though not the most prominent) gas-holder blew a hole in it and set the gas on fire; fortunately there was no explosion. In 1976, three intruders carrying a bomb set it off, accidentally, beside No 6 gas-holder; all three were killed by the fireball resulting from the ignition of gas released by the fracture; but again there was no explosion. If there had been on either occasion, not much of the gasworks, or very likely of the populous Markets district, would have been left.

Belfast is exceptionally rich in architectural sculpture. Thomas Fitzpatrick, a really remarkable working sculptor, was certainly responsible for the Red Indian at 36 Victoria Street (Pl. 36) and the Chinaman round the corner in Marlborough Street (Pl. 38); possibly also for the engineer Stevenson (Pl. 37) and the poet Tom Moore (Pl. 39) in Linen Hall Street.

36

37

38

39

40

Thomas Fitzpatrick was the author of all the sculpture on the Head Office of the Ulster Bank (Pl. 40), designed by James Hamilton and completed in 1860; perhaps for the pediment of the Ulster Brewery in Sandy Row—demolished to make way for a community centre, (Pl. 41); certainly for the semi-caryatid Continents of 36 Victoria Street (Pl. 44) and for the pediment of the Custom-House (Pl. 45).

Victoria and Albert loom large in the iconography of Belfast. Pl. 42: Albert, in garter robes on the Albert Clock, is by S. F. Lynn. Pl. 43: The Queen, in frothy lace, stood in Durham Street—the building was demolished, the statue (by John Cassidy) rescued and in the care of the National Trust.

Both visited Belfast on 11th August 1849: the accompanying commemorative lines are 'from the pen of a respected citizen'.

41

She came in the grace of her
  womanly love,
The Irishman's ardent
  affections to move;
His Cushla machree
Filled her heart with such glee,
That oft, to her Albert, she
  said with delight—
'His head may be wrong, but
  his heart's in the right'.

Hurrah for the Queen! may
  posterity see
Each year on this island a
  grand jubilee:
May Minstrels arise
To contend for the prize;
And bards, yet unborn, sing
  the joys of the past—
OF VICTORIA, and ALBERT,
  and loyal Belfast.

43

44

45

46

47

Victorian ironwork is often richly effective. Pl. 46: The elaborate glass and iron pub-sign of *The Morning Star* in Pottinger's Entry. Pls. 47 and 48: The railings and lamp standards of the Ulster Bank were designed by the architect James Hamilton of Glasgow, and cast for him there by Messrs. Laidlaw.

48

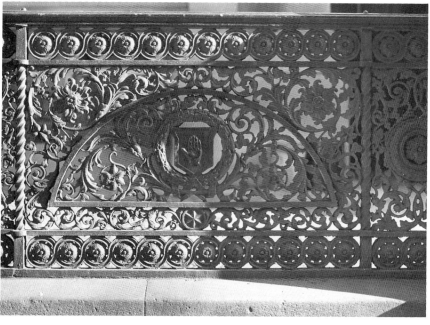

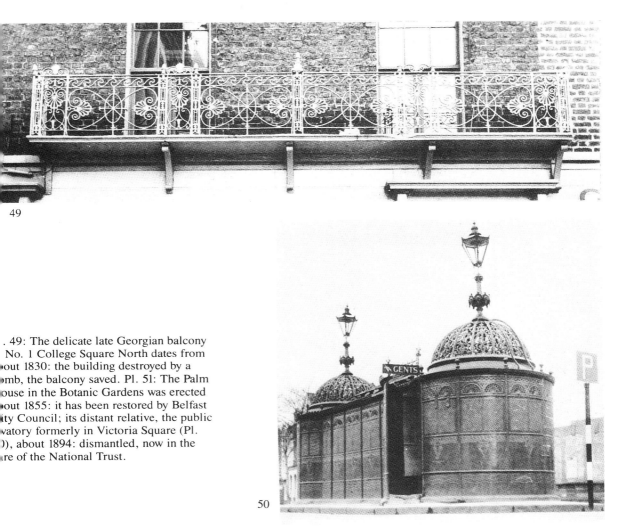

49

Pl. 49: The delicate late Georgian balcony
of No. 1 College Square North dates from
about 1830: the building destroyed by a
bomb, the balcony saved. Pl. 51: The Palm
House in the Botanic Gardens was erected
about 1855: it has been restored by Belfast
City Council; its distant relative, the public
lavatory formerly in Victoria Square (Pl.
50), about 1894: dismantled, now in the
care of the National Trust.

50

51

52

53

Not every Victorian building was ornate: Alex McAllister designed both the simplified-Gothic Oxford Street schools (restored and now used as warehouses) (Pl. 52); and the nearby naïve-nautical chandler's store (Pl. 53). The old Town Hall in Victoria Street, designed by Thomas Jackson & Son in 1871 (Pl. 54) was severely criticized for its over-simplicity and lack of ostentation. It has recently been restored to provide a new Recorder's Court.

54

55

W. H. Lynn, one of the few Belfast architects to be widely employed outside Ireland, relied more on austere massing than on ornament. Pl. 55: Belfast Castle was completed in 1870; the garden staircase (see Pl. 62) was a later addition. Now undergoing extensive restoration. Pl. 56: This old photograph shows the full majesty of Richardson Sons and Owden's warehouse in its original setting, and before its roof was blown off by war-time bombs. Recently restored by Marks & Spencer, the tall roof replaced but not the chimneys or dormers.

56

57

Pl. 57: St Matthew's, Woodvale Road, is a most unusual trefoil church. Old Irish Round Tower and all, it is built of yellow brick, the treads of the tower staircase being indicated on the outside by courses of red brick.

Few have any architectural merit, though some are impressive by virtue of their massive scale.

Plain engineering works there were, of course, in plenty. The river Lagan was straightened, docks, quays, and a great part of the present shipyard were constructed. The Alexandra Graving Dock, designed by Redfern Kelly and T. R. Salmond, was opened in 1889. The Lagan Railway Bridge was built between 1870 and 1875, probably by Telford McNeill, son of the great railway engineer: it seems to come straight out of a child's Hornby set, and is correspondingly endearing.[70] The Albert Bridge dates from 1890, replacing the earlier bridge of the same name which had collapsed, and was designed by J. C. Bretland, the City Surveyor. It is a bridge without lightness, and seems really to groan beneath the traffic.

The other public buildings of the last quarter of the century are not, in the main, of much distinction. One exception was the original Water Commissioner's office in Royal Avenue (completed 1883; demolished 1966), an excellent Palladian building of red stone, with polished granite Corinthian engaged columns, designed by the very scholarly architect W. J. Fennell, and his first major commission. It was alleged that he secured it by unfair means, and that his design was a plagiarism of a sketch previously prepared by one of the Commissioners; it was adopted in preference to the original first choice of the Board; and nine of the fifteen competitors signed an indignant petition for an inquiry into the conduct of the competition: but without result. Fennell also designed special boardroom furniture for the Commissioners, some of which survives. The Head Post Office,[71] a grimly machicolated building in Royal Avenue, was built in 1886 by James Owen of the Board of Public Works (Charles Lanyon's brother-in-law). Contemporaries considered this 'a capital building', and so does Mr John Betjeman, but others find it too gloomy and mistrustful. It is built of local stone, and it is curious that, almost alone in Belfast, it has acquired a velvety Black Country grime. Recent Post Office improvements include an enormous raw concrete slab around the main doorway, and garish yellow paint in the window-frames.

The Reform Club, also in Royal Avenue, was built in 1883 by Maxwell and Tuke of Manchester; a slap in the eye for the local architects, but nothing to the shock in store for those local Reformers who supported Mr Gladstone and Home Rule: for three years later the club excluded all but 'Liberal Unionists', whatever they may be, and still does.[72]

All these buildings in Royal Avenue formed part of a notable piece of town planning. The expansion of Belfast had gone largely uncontrolled, apart from the bye-laws (which at least secured Belfast from the back-to-back housing endured by the citizens of some industrial cities). In the 1880s a determined attempt was made to tidy up some of the older and more bedraggled parts of the town. The alleys of Hercules Street were swept away. As a slightly caustic article on Belfast in the eleventh edition of the *Encyclopaedia Brittanica*, from an unknown pen, remarked, 'The appearance of the city plainly demonstrates the modern growth of its importance, and evidence is not wanting that for a considerable period

---

[70] Replaced on the building of the new central railway station in 1976: the new stucture just as simple and uncomplicated as the old: by Randal, Palmer & Tritton, the very same firm that acted at engineers for the construction of the original Boyne Viaduct.

[71] Sold for demolition in 1985; inexplicably, never listed for preservation. One of the buildings which I have come to admire more: today, I should award it two, if not three, stars. See Brian Walker and Hugh Dixon *No Mean City* (Belfast, 1983), p. 66. Stop press: demolished June 1985.

[72] No longer: as a result of successive amalgamations, the political qualifications have been dropped from its constitution. Its remarkable billiard-room may now be admired by members of all parties, or none.

architectural improvement was unable to keep pace with commercial development. Many squalid districts, however, have been improved away to make room for new thoroughfares and handsome buildings. One thoroughfare thus constructed is the finest in Belfast—Royal Avenue! [73]

It was planned as a composite whole; the Corporation acquired the entire site, and then let it off for building subject to rigid controls over heights and elevations. Though few of the individual buildings were distinguished, the result was coherent and had a very definite canyon-like character of its own, first seriously breached by demolitions in 1966.[74] A similar but much less successful scheme was undertaken in Ormeau Avenue in 1884.

Other public ventures of this period include St George's Markets in May Street, and the Fish Market in Oxford Street, both [75] by J. C. Bretland, the former in 1890, the latter 1896: admirable adaptations of classical motifs to utilitarian needs. They are cheap, practical, yet handsome; today neglected—many knops are missing, and there are corrugated iron partitions inside. The radial grilles of ironwork in the archways are an extremely effective variant on the fanlight principle. The Morgue [76] in Laganbank Road, also by J. C. Bretland, is a very discreet brick building, with terra-cotta panels of festoons; but no urns. The Public Baths in Peter's Hill (by William Hastings, 1879; demolished 1966) and in Ormeau Avenue (by R. Watt, 1888) were both regrettable brick buildings markedly inferior both in dignity and in voluptuousness to the baths of ancient Rome. The Power Station [77] in East Bridge Street, built in 1898 by Graeme Watt and Tulloch, is a curious piece of Industrial Romantic building, described at the time as 'English Renaissance'; it is a novel effort, with arcades, rustications, and a great knobbly gateway. One of the most evocative buildings of the period is the headquarters of the Belfast Tramway Company,[78] in Napier Street off the Sandy Row, a red brick palace with stabling for 312 horses, now sadly fallen from its former splendour; it was designed in 1899 by the Secretary of the Tramway Company, Andrew Nance, CE.

I have left until last the buildings of W. H. Lynn, whose achievements as the leading Belfast practitioner span the last quarter of the century. In 1868 he built the new library for the Queen's College; an extremely intellectual, if somewhat impractical, design in red and black brick, the window details French, the five cross-gables German Gothic.[79] The building is now overshadowed by a towering contemporary stack, and is shortly to be demolished.[80] In 1869 he was busy with Belfast Castle, and with Richardson Sons and Owden's warehouse. In 1871 he built St James' church; in 1872 Carlisle Memorial Methodist Church. He was kept busy throughout the 1870s with the Château St Louis in Quebec, and Ballymena Castle. In 1885 he worked on St Andrew's Church, Dublin; in the later 1880s he was busy on the Belfast Public Library in Royal Avenue. This is an impressive classical building, executed in red sandstone especially imported from Scotland, and the subject-matter of prolonged

73   *Encyclopaedia Britannica*, 11th ed., 1910, Vol 3, p. 664.
74   Its integrity has been much prejudiced by bombs, fires, and inappropriate redevelopments; and is now under even greater threat.
75   Now both in poor shape, knocked about both by bombs and vandals; the Fish Market clock has gone; more than half the knops are missing; a good many of the openings have been blocked up.
76   Demolished.
77   Demolished; only a very long stone wall (in need of repair) and three ornamental gate-pillars survive: but they are worth keeping.
78   Demolished.
79   T. W. Moody and J. C. Beckett, *Queen's Belfast, 1845-1949: the History of a University* (London, 1959), Vol I, p. 151.
80   Happily, reprieved and the exterior well restored; the interior rather cleverly modernised.

strikes: it has a formal Corinthian portico of columns and pilasters, freely adorned with swags and rustications. The interior is liberally be-sprinkled with Ionic columns, save for the rather splendid domed reference library, which is Corinthian. Recently cleaned and restored, it constitutes an interesting reversion by Lynn to the earlier style of Lanyon; unfortunately it seems a little top-heavy, and a little too self-conscious to be entirely successful.

In 1893 Lynn built the Royal Bank, Dame Street, Dublin, and in the following year the utilitarian Tudor red-brick of Campbell College, Belfast. He was also engaged in additions to the Harbour Office, and in the final despoliation of Sir Robert Taylor's work in the Belfast Bank. In 1900, when he was seventy-one, he undertook the design of the new department store of Messrs Robertson Ledlie Ferguson in Castle Place, still known (after the eighteenth-century building formerly on the same site) as the Bank Buildings.[81] In the previous five years, Young and Mackenzie had tried to repeat their popular success at Robinson and Cleaver's for Messrs Anderson and McAuley. The result, at 1-7 Donegall Place, is comparatively insipid; even the carving is less good; twenty-nine assorted and truncated ladies and gentlemen, some crowned, others not, smirk, gape or simper down from above the first-floor windows. Despite his years, Lynn was determined to produce a building more appropriate to the new century. The Bank Buildings do, indeed, constitute a bridge to the twentieth century. Their framed construction made a new style possible; and Lynn chose rather a successful compromise between a classical style in the upper part of the building and a great expanse of plate glass below. The effect is somewhat spoiled, however, by the way in which, of the six great Corinthian columns which rise through the third and fourth storeys, numbers two and five are carried, through the second and ground floors, apparently, on strips of bronze about three inches wide—a most alarming and vertiginous feature of an otherwise dignified design. Nevertheless Lynn had demonstrated once again his ability to move, however austerely and disconcertingly, with the times.

[81] Now refurbished under new ownership; with most unfortunate pink-eyed new windows, however.

FIVE

THE EDWARDIAN CITY

1900–1914

There are three major monuments of Edwardian architecture in Belfast: one secular, the City Hall; and two religious, great temples of Protestantism, Belfast Cathedral and the Assembly's Building of the Presbyterian Church. To appreciate the full significance of these elaborate and ambitious fanes, it is necessary to see them in their historical context; and to look back at the development of Belfast, which had attained the status of a City in 1888.

The increase in its population in the course of the nineteenth century had been phenomenal. In 1800 the figure had stood at just over 20,000; in 1831, 50,000; in 1861, 120,000; in 1891, when for the first time it outstripped Dublin, 250,000; by 1901, it had reached 350,000.[1] Obviously, this rate of increase placed a great strain on the administration and public services of the city; at the same time, gridirons of working-class housing spread swiftly outwards from the city centre in every direction—up the hillsides towards the Antrim escarpment, across the slob and mudflats of Ballymacarrett. The new arrivals came to the city to escape the Famine and the long years of agricultural depression which followed it; they were drawn by the great expansion of industry in and around Belfast. The linen trade had flourished ever since the setback to cotton caused by the American Civil War; the shipyard was now building the largest transatlantic liners in the world for the White Star line.

The influx set up new tensions. In 1800 Catholics amounted to no more than six per cent of the town's population; by the end of the century they made up thirty-four per cent of the total. More and more the Protestants of Belfast and the North-East drew away from their fellow-Irishmen elsewhere. Catholic emancipation had been granted in 1829. The disestablishment of the Church of Ireland followed in 1871; Mr Gladstone introduced his first Home Rule Bill in 1886. In that year, Lord Randolph Churchill first 'played the Orange card'; he visited Belfast, and greatly inflamed Protestant feelings; it was he who shortly after announced that 'Ulster would fight, and Ulster would be right'. And fighting there was, of a kind: religious rioting in Belfast has ever since been a recurring feature of the city's social life. There were riots in 1872; 1884; 1886; 1907; 1909; 1920, and the following years; 1936; 1964 and 1966. These troubles were, and are, the symptoms of a division within the community; but they represent also the deep division which split Protestant Ulster, and its kernel Belfast, from the rest of Ireland. Rightly or wrongly, the dominant majority in

1   D. J. Owen, *History of Belfast* (Belfast, 1921), p. 379.

Belfast felt itself more and more threatened and beleaguered by the dominant majority in Ireland as a whole. The uneducated might express their views by rioting, but the Belfast Chamber of Commerce sent a deputation to wait on Mr Gladstone and point out to him that its members were poorer by thousands of pounds owing to the fall in Irish stocks consequent upon the introduction of his second Home Rule Bill.[2] From 1886 onwards, Protestant Belfast was on the defensive; but it came to have a new sense of its separate identity. No longer was Belfast content to be the second city of Ireland; subjectively it saw itself both as a great industrial centre, and as the religious and political capital of the Protestant and Unionist North-East. There were still moderate Liberals, and there were by now Labour and trade union leaders, active in Belfast; there was a substantial minority in favour of Home Rule; but they were swept aside in a great tide of emotional separatism which led to the gun-runnings at Larne and Howth, the fanaticism of the Ulster Volunteer Force and of the Irish Republican Army, the signing of the covenant, the establishment of a separate Parliament in Ulster, and all the unhappy events associated with the foundation of Northern Ireland as a separate entity having its centre of gravity in Belfast.

As the capital of a subordinate Government, Belfast has two architectural monuments of consequence, both too recent to be easily judged: the Houses of Parliament at Stormont, designed by Sir Arnold Thornely and completed in 1932; and the Royal Courts of Justice, designed by J. G. West and completed in 1933. It seems to me that the City Hall, the Cathedral and the Assembly's Building must be viewed in the same light; architecturally, they constitute the corporate expression of embattled Unionism, and of an effort (perhaps largely unconscious) to convert a brash and sprawling industrial centre into a politico-religious capital city.

Of the three, Belfast City Hall is aesthetically by far the most successful. Although the   ***
Town Hall had been completed as recently as 1871, only seventeen years later negotiations for a new site were in hand. The White Linen Hall in Donegall Square was no longer serving the purpose for which it had been built, and the Countess of Shaftesbury started legal proceedings to regain possession of the site. It seems that her (very reasonable) intention was that the ground should be laid out as a public garden. There is no doubt of the want of an open space near the City's centre; but the Corporation (also reasonably) argued that no other suitable site for a City Hall was available. A settlement was come to, the old Linen Hall was demolished in 1896, and later that year a competition was held, the Assessors being Alfred Waterhouse (then President of the RIBA) and J. C. Bretland, the City Surveyor. The plans submitted by Alfred Brumwell Thomas, a young London architect aged thirty-one, were chosen. Thomas was knighted on the completion of the building in 1906. His other principal works were the Town Halls of Stockport, Woolwich and Clacton. He died only in 1948. (The offices of the Mersey Docks and Harbour Board on the waterfront at Liverpool—started in 1907, completed in 1913 [3]—are a *very* close relative of the City Hall; curiously, they were designed by Arnold Thornely who was afterwards the architect of the Parliament Buildings at Stormont.)

Many citizens of Belfast have become accustomed to laughing at their City Hall, but indeed it is no laughing matter. It is a remarkable building, and one which in a number of respects, though not in all, is extremely successful (Plates 65 and 67). It comprises a large quadrilateral of Portland stone, 300 feet in width, ranged round a central courtyard; at the centre there

[2]   H. C. Plunkett, *Ireland in the New Century* (London, 1904), p. 67.
[3]   Quentin Hughes, *Seaport* (London, 1964), pp 73-4.

is a great Ionic dome 173 feet high; at each corner there is a smaller tower and subsidiary dome. The front, though impressive, is somewhat over-decorated, depending on a rhythm of coupled Ionic columns; the central portico and pediment are largely masked by the peculiar and ugly porte-cochère, and the free-standing statue of Queen Victoria in front of it. Indeed this was recognised very early on as the weak point in the whole composition. When the scaffolding came down in 1905, the *Irish Builder's* correspondent wrote: 'All are giving each other guesses as to the nature of the erection in front of the centre. Some guess it to be a porte-cochère, but these are jokers ... The majority incline to consider it a mausoleum for the statue of Queen Victoria which, she not liking, stepped out of, with her pedestal, to the open ground'.[8]

The stone statue of Queen Victoria is by Thomas Brock, RA, as are her bronze supporters representing Spinning and Shipbuilding. She was unveiled by her son, King Edward VII, on 27 July 1903; according to a barely credible account in the *Belfast News Letter*, he looked back over his shoulder at his Mamma as the carriage was receding after the ceremony, and exclaimed 'Couldn't be better!'[5]

The pediment carving was designed by Frederick Pomeroy, and partly executed by him and partly by the local carver J. Edgar Winter. It is spirited if much overcrowded: the subject-matter is Hibernia encouraging and promoting the commerce and arts of the City: she is supported by Minerva, Industry, Labour, Liberty, and a variety of persons symbolic of different branches of Commerce, clutching appropriate harps, torches, bolts of linen, spinning-wheels and so forth. All the carving is now extremely grubby; only Hibernia's hand, clutching a flaming torch, protrudes through the pigeon-netting, like the hand of a desperate prisoner thrust between the bars.

The side elevations are both simpler and more satisfactory; the windows rise through three storeys, not two; and, apart from the central projections, the walls are articulated with pilasters not pillars. The back view is the most satisfactory of all; there is a strength and simplicity about the design of the rear portico (and especially the swashbuckling vigour of the carving around the *oeil-de-boeuf* in the pediment) which lends real dignity to the design. It is genuinely impressive when seen down the canyon of Linen Hall Street early on a sunny morning.

Although the exterior of the City Hall is somewhat over-ornate, and although neither the corner towers nor the porte-cochère are entirely successful, yet the overall effect is very imposing. No building could better have symbolized the pretensions of the Edwardian city. From far and near, the dome floats above the roof-tops, like a light-buoy marking out the centre of Belfast.

The interior is ornate in a moderately restrained way. There is much streaky and blotchy marble; a great semi-circular stair-well below the dome; and there is a great deal of very heavy-handed but effective rococo plasterwork. The Banqueting Hall was blitzed, but has been restored. The grounds, a small island of greenery in the city centre, enshrine a number of endearing monuments. There are highly municipal statues of four local worthies, Sir Edward Harland, shipbuilder, by Thomas Brock; Sir James Haslett, druggist, by Pomeroy; Sir Dan Dixon, builder's provider, in bronze, by Sir Hamo Thorneycroft; and Sir Robert McMordie, solicitor, also by Pomeroy. There are memorials to those who were killed in the Boer War (by Sydney March), and to those who were drowned in the *Titanic* on her maiden voyage (by Brock). The cenotaph and Garden of Remembrance are by Brumwell

4   *Irish Builder*, 1905, p. 694.   5   *Belfast News Letter*, 28 July 1903.

Thomas. Much the finest, however, is the Memorial to the first Marquis of Dufferin (Plate   ***
72). This local baron-made-good had in early life written the charming *Letters from High
Latitudes*, and became successively Governor-General of Canada, ambassador to Russia,
to Turkey, and Viceroy of India. His latter years were clouded by his involvement in the
financial scandal surrounding the bankruptcy and suicide of Whitaker Wright, and the
collapse of the London and Globe Finance Corporation. His memorial, jointly composed
by Brumwell Thomas and Frederick Pomeroy, makes no allusion to this unfortunate episode;
but the delightfully imperial pose of the vice-regal old gentleman is admirably set off by
his supporters—a sabre'd and turbanned Indian sitting on a cannon, and a snowshoe'd and
musketed Canadian sitting on a dead moose—and by the frolicsome little temple, a tiny
version of the City Hall, in which he is enshrined.

The ultimate cost of the City Hall was over £360,000. Of this total a staggering proportion
must have been spent on ornament in one form or another; the marble work cost £21,681;
carving and sculpture, £9,817; plasterwork, £7,164; and stained glass £1,556.[6] Whether the
ratepayers of any city today would stand for similar expenditure must be more than doubtful;
but clearly the citizens of 1906, when the City Hall was completed, were pleased with the
splendiferous edifice they had purchased. One unhappy episode marred the conclusion of the
undertaking: in the spring of 1907 Sir Brumwell Thomas was obliged to issue a writ for   ✂
£13,000 odd, the balance of his fees.[7]

Mention should be made of the extraordinary triple-branched lamp-posts which are erected
outside the house of the Lord Mayor for the time being (Plate 64). Their history is mysterious;
the Corporation has lost all records of their origin; but it seems likely that these ceremonial
candelabra (serving a purpose not dissimilar to that of the star at Bethlehem) were installed
for the first time on the completion of the City Hall, outside which there stands a similar
pair. The enormous standards with their square holders contrast unfavourably with Victorian
ironwork. They have been converted from gas to electricity, and are now painted a greasy
gilt colour. They are adorned with sailing-ships and sea-horses, and each post is propped
up by four cretinous putti, coy and obscene: one holding a model boat in his hand: one
reading a book he has just finished printing: one holding a trowel and spirit-level, and
unclothed save for an immodest masonic apron: one idle and empty-handed, leaning cross-
legged against his spinning-wheel.

The proposal that Belfast should have a Protestant Cathedral originated in 1895. The
decision to go ahead was taken in the following year. At that time the diocese of Down and
Connor and Dromore was united under a single Bishop; there were already three Cathedrals
in the diocese, all of very respectable antiquity, at Downpatrick, Lisburn and Dromore.
It seems at no time seriously to have been proposed that Belfast should be constitued a new
diocese; but since a cathedral church is, by definition, that in which a bishop sets his cathedra
or throne, the venture was from the outset a slightly illogical one. Only three new cathedrals
had then been built in the British Isles since the Reformation,[8] in London, Truro and Cork.
Coventry and Liverpool lay in the future. The great industrial cities of England and Scotland
had enlarged or adapted their parish churches as need dictated. But the churchmen of Belfast
determined upon a fourth cathedral in their diocese, which should at the same time be the
Parish Church of Belfast.

---

6   *Irish Builder*, 1907, p. 501.   7   *Ibid.*, p. 286.
8   Not true; I cannot remember where I picked up this exaggerated claim; I think it must have been
from the rhetoric of some over-excited clergyman of the day.

The reasons given for this decision seem questionable. In the original appeal for funds, it was suggested that 'its erection on the site proposed, which is about the very centre of the city, cannot fail to exert a wholesome moral influence on a district whose present condition is by no means satisfactory'.[9] It is doubtful if, in this respect, the hopes of its proponents have been realized. The appeal was boosted by a passionate speech in the Ulster Hall by the leading opponent of Welsh disestablishment, the Archbishop of Canterbury, Archbishop Benson, in which he congratulated the assembled clergy and laity upon 'the grand way in which you met the calamity'—disestablishment—'which we do not intend to fall upon us'.[10] Two days later, over-tired by his exertions in Ireland, he died at morning service in Hawarden parish church while on a visit to Mr Gladstone.

For their site the cathedralizers chose the old parish church of St Anne. Its demolition seems to have been no more lamented than the destruction of Taylor's Assembly Rooms; Georgian architecture was as little regarded in the 1890s as Victorian architecture is now.[11] For their architects they chose two distinguished alumni of Lanyon, Thomas Drew and W. H. Lynn. The latter, however, tactfully withdrew into the background: 'These gentlemen, after conference and consultation, agreed upon the general features of the proposed Church ... Mr Lynn subsequently, however, while expressing his willingness to continue to advise generally in the matter, elected to leave the more responsible duty of preparing the design for the building in the hands of Mr Drew'.[12]

Drew's original plans were for a very orthodox Gothic cathedral, with a large rose window at the West end, a square tower at the crossing, and a ribbed stone roof. However, after publication of the prospectus, he revised his drawings and settled for a simplified Romanesque style, retaining however some features of the original, with a wooden ceiling.

Work on the nave continued until Drew's death in 1910. Lynn carried on until he, too, died in 1915. From 1915 to 1922 Dr McGregor Chalmers; for 1922 to 1924 R. M. Close; from 1924 to 1948 Sir Charles Nicholson; from 1948 to 1963, his partner, T. J. Rushton; and subsequently John McGeagh, have carried on the work.[13] The cathedrals of the middle ages were built by successive generations of craftsmen over very long periods; but in the middle ages architectural styles and materials changed less swiftly than they have done so far in this century. The still uncompleted cathedral presents in consequence a disconcerting confusion of styles.

** The nave itself, as designed by Drew, is the most successful part; it is enormously tall, plain and simple: massive, brooding and impressive. The nave columns and corbels have rather unexpected symbolic carvings by Morris Harding. Each capital is devoted to a theme; they include Womanhood, Shipbuilding, and (of all things) Freemasonry. For some reason, miniature busts of Lloyd George and Asquith count as Shipbuilding. The Irish Protestant worthies in the corbels include Bishop Berkeley and Mrs C. F. Alexander, author of 'There is a green hill far away'.[14]

---

9   *A Cathedral for Belfast* (Belfast, 1896), p. 10.
10 Speech in Ulster Hall, 9 October 1896.
11 The box-pews from old St Anne's are said to have been bought by a dealer named McIlwaine and turned into dining-room tables.
12 *A Cathedral for Belfast* (Belfast, 1896), p. 6.
13 And more recently, Robert McKinstry.
14 J. A. Young, *Unfinished Pilgrimage* (undated), passim.

By virtue of a special Act of Parliament, Lord Carson lies buried in the South aisle.

The West front, which represents a major departure from the intentions of Drew and Lynn, was completed as a War Memorial (at the suggestion of Carson) in 1927. It constitutes a remarkable anthology of architectural styles; the columns supporting the portal employ almost every idiom known to Gothic and Romanesque, plus Corinthian pilasters. The carvings in the tympana, by Esmond Burton, are unimpressive. Rather sensible revolving doors, as used in department stores, lead to the interior; to the left is the Chapel of the Holy Spirit, the work of Nicholson; to the right, the baptistery, designed by Lynn, with a fine mosaic roof.

The crossing, transepts and tower are as yet unbuilt; there are inoffensive temporary plain walls behind the choir. The East end has been completed to the original dimensions, but in a chunky and uncomfortable (though rather clever) compromise between the Edwardian and contemporary styles.[15] The Ambulatory is fitted up as a kind of museum; it contains one good piece of Irish Chippendale—the chair used in old St Anne's by the Sovereign of Belfast, predecessor of the mayor—and a very ornate presentation grandfather clock. The pulpit, a present from Westminster Abbey, was designed by Sir George Gilbert Scott in 1863; it is pleasant to record that Harry Hems carved the capitals on it in his youth.[16]

Altogether, the Cathedral, unfinished as it is, is an unsatisfactory edifice; and the problem of welding its disparate parts into a harmonious whole seems an insoluble one.[17] It is possible at any rate to sympathize profoundly with those whose duty it is to make the attempt.

In 1900, Sir Thomas Drew was appointed Assessor in the competition for the design of a new Church House and Assembly Hall to be erected for the Presbyterian Church in Ireland on the site of the old Fisherwick Church, that congregation having built itself a Church on the Malone Road to designs by S. P. Close. There followed one of the most resounding rows in architectural history. Various thunderous leaders appeared in the *Irish Builder*, and in the *British Architect*; and several acid letters. The original conditions, it appears, had been drawn up by Robert Young as architect to the Presbyterian Church. It was laid down that the buildings, which were to contain specified accommodation, should cost no more than £30,000. A number of entries were received; but Sir Thomas Drew concluded that compliance with this condition was impracticable, and the competition was abortive, though a young architect named Savage obtained first place. Indeed, Drew described the conditions as being 'in terms of unusual stringency, a distasteful and impossible task'. Instead of revising the terms of the competition, the Church authorities, astoundingly, appointed Robert Young and his partner Mackenzie to erect the buildings as specified—which they did, 'at a cost

[15] The crossing was completed to Rushton's designs; the south transept, in 1974, by John McGeagh; and the north transept in 1981, to McGeagh's designs, under the supervision of Robert McKinstry. The modest Romanesque spire now in course of erection (on an uncomfortably constricted base) is to Robert McKinstry's design. Appeal brochure, *Belfast Cathedral* (Belfast, 1985). On the whole, the work carried out over the past eighteen years has been both rather clever, and rather successful. There are a few jarring notes: I do not care for the obstrusive tie-beams and king-posts in the transept arches; the cantilevered concrete platform on which the organ stands is also disconcerting.

[16] *Irish Builder*, 1910, p. 386. This pulpit was destroyed by fire in a Belfast store en route to the Church of the Incarnation, Dallas, Texas. It had been thrown out 'because it would not be in keeping with' the cathedral as completed: yet the new pulpit which replaced it is even more unsuitable.

[17] In retrospect, the successive cathedral architects have come surprisingly close to solving the insoluble.

of about £70,000'.[18]

The Presbyterians, in an unparalleled stroke of ecclesiastical one-upmanship, sought to redress the adverse balance of publicity by letting it be known that the angel's faces on the building were being 'specially copied from life'.[19]

When the buildings were opened in 1905, some of the comments were understandably hostile, and due allowance must be made for professional jealousy. There was criticism of the 'Tudor Style, with its sprawling senile arches that resemble nothing so much as a nonagenarian on crutches, its superficial meretriciousness of ornament, its lifeless formalism . . . Standing at a distance . . . one's mind gathers the impression that [the buildings] were designed of greater height, to occupy less space, and had somehow been sat on so that they might squelch out and fill all the interstices of a building front commercially valuable . . . A church is worldly enough to be desirous of pay, but it is unwise to be clamant of it . . . instead of receding, the new buildings make bay window bids for notice'.[20] Despite its indignation, the general conclusion of the *Irish Builder* that the interior was successful, the general design not, seems sound. A curious glass-roofed ambulatory-cum-foyer leads into the hall itself; the latter is polygonal, with two tiers of balconies within a Tudor framework, and *art nouveau* glass in the central roof-light.

In fact, this harsh and craggy pile of blackened Scottish-Tudor stone is one of the less attractive buildings of Belfast.[21] It is surmounted by a rather squat tower, with two high balconies, topped with a Gothic crown reminiscent of that on St Giles in Edinburgh. There are great recessed oriel windows above the main doorway; and there is much curious carving, of very uneven quality, partly by Edgar Winter and partly by Purdy and Millard. The themes include a number of dragons, apparently expiring in agony, and a very sick eagle in deepest moult, as well as a great number of cherubim and seraphim with coyly drooping eyelids.

During these same years, Young and Mackenzie had been busy on two of the enormous office blocks which lend, at any rate, variety to Donegall Square; no city can have a formal centre more variegated than that of Belfast. The largest of these is the Scottish Provident Institution, an immense towering Corinthian block of now blackened Giffnock sandstone [22] (Plate 66). It was built in sections between 1899 and 1902, and is faintly reminiscent of the work of Cuthbert Brodrick in Leeds. The central bay is bowed; there are six floors and an attic storey; heavy engaged Corinthian columns run through the third, fourth and fifth floors. The octagonal domes at the corners, with heavy knops, are not very successful. The whole building is terribly heavy both in mass and in detail. The original voluminous decoration has now been subordinated to the mass by all-pervading grime and starling-droppings; there are two large sphinxes, four dolphins, sixteen lion's heads, and seventeen queens; four panels showing printing, ropemaking, shipbuilding, and spinning, all being carried on by amoretti; and at the corner of Wellington Place, a rather nauseating marble group in a pompous aedicule comprising a semi-nude lady doing her hair; a small boy imitating her; and another lady looking on in surprise: apparently modelled on 'the beautiful seal' of the Scottish Provident Institution. All the carvings are by Purdy and Millard.

The Ocean Buildings, completed in 1902 by the same firm, are quite another cup of tea. Carried out in the Scottish-Baronial-Tudor style in very pink sandstone,[23] their five storeys

18 *Irish Builder*, 1900, pp 530, 555-6; 1905, p. 406.   19 *Ibid.*, 1905, p. 194.
20 *Ibia.*, p. 406.
21 Repeatedly damaged by fire and bombs, it has been well restored.
22 Underpinned, and the stonework cleaned, in 1981.
23 The stonework well cleaned in 1982.

rear up an odd and asymmetrical skyline. There are heavy projecting oriels, and a rather curious corner doorway: above it the heads of Edward VII, Queen Victoria, and Queen Alexandra groan under the weight they have to carry (Plate 69). There are many good grotesques and gargoyles, carved with much spirit by Winter and Thompson. The Northern Bank on the opposite side of the square is another work of Young and Mackenzie, completed in 1903;[24] a tall narrow building in red-brick Jacobethan style, with much armorial stone-carving, and the signs of the Zodiac dividing the first floor from the second floor oriels; all carved by Purdy and Millard.

Another large office block, this time in Donegall Square South, is that of the Scottish Temperance Buildings, completed in 1904 to plans by Henry Seaver. It is a very bulging building of pink stone, 'a fine and well-proportioned design, a free treatment of the Scottish Baronial style';[25] to present-day eyes, the combination of fourth-floor arcades and château-type turrets, with mock-Jacobean fenestration in flat panels, is almost unbearable. No. 36 Donegall Place is a strange but rather charming building in a wobbly baroque style designed by Vincent Craig (an elder brother of Lord Craigavon) for Sharman D. Neill, the leading firm of clockmakers, now defunct; the façade includes a shallow pediment, carved by Winter and Thompson, in which two elongated horizontal ladies are apparently trying to seduce Father Time. The whole building, of cream-painted brick, has very decided character; it was completed in 1903.

Although the office blocks in the very centre of the city must loom large in any account of Edwardian development, a number of public buildings were erected during this period. The Mater Infirmorum Hospital, on the Crumlin Road, was completed in 1900 to plans by W. J. Fennell; a rather depressing exercise in sub-Tudor red brick. Fennell was also the architect of the (now abandoned) Maternity Hospital in Townsend Street,[26] opened in 1904. It must have been a source of irritation to him that outsiders were brought in to design the much larger Royal Victoria Hospital on the Grosvenor Road, which is the work of Henman and Cooper of Birmingham; the Commitee inspected several English hospitals, and was impressed by the work of William Henman, who had built the Birmingham General Hospital. The foundations were laid in 1901; the unusual design (no windows and no direct open-air ventilation in the wards) was described by critical medical men at the time as 'a cross between a factory and a gaol'. In fact, a system of forced draught ventilation was deliberately adopted to minimize the risk of infection; according to informed opinion in 1900, 'it approaches as nearly perfection as is possible under human conditions'.[27]

The building of the Technical College in College Square caused substantial heart-burnings. Its deplorable siting was the outcome of the financial embarrassment of the Governors of the Royal Belfast Academical Institution. They had long been in debt; and in 1899 resolved on the extreme measure of realizing the site value of parts of the grounds surrounding the school. One section was let off for the Whitla Medical Institute (built by W. J. Fennell in 1902); a substantial part in front of the main range of buildings was leased in 1900 to the Belfast Corporation at a rent of £1,350. The resulting building masks Soane's façade of the school, overshadows it, and generally presents an outstanding example of egregious town planning.

As if the demerits of the site were not enough, there was serious trouble both over the ✂

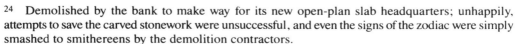

24 Demolished by the bank to make way for its new open-plan slab headquarters; unhappily, attempts to save the carved stonework were unsuccessful, and even the signs of the zodiac were simply smashed to smithereens by the demolition contractors.
25 *Irish Builder*, 1904, p. 302.   26 Demolished.   27 *Irish Builder*, 1900, pp 247-8.

choice of architect and over the choice of style. In 1900, the Editor of the *Irish Builder* was constrained to write: 'Belfast seems destined to preserve an unenviable notoriety in the matter of questionable architectural methods', apropos of the attempt by a few councillors 'by a scratch vote and a narrow majority', quietly to appoint Mr Samuel Stevenson, architect of Gallaher's enormous factory, to design the Technical College without a competition.[28] Soon afterwards the report of his appointment was confirmed. On its completion in 1907, the building was attacked as a straight crib from the War Office in London, a deplorable building designed in 1898 by William Young, and completed after his death by his son in the same year as the Technical College.[29] 'Its likeness to the principal façade of the new War Office . . . is almost indistinguishable, but for certain architectural faults which the War Office lacks, such as the superimposure of the double columns of the angle turrets on a vertical line of fenestration . . . The dominant impression is of utility rather than of beauty'.[30] In fact, the siting is so distressing that it is barely possible to judge the merits of the Technical College impartially; it is the largest and most ornate cuckoo's egg ever laid in songbird's nest. But even if it were ideally sited, it is doubtful if its proportions or detailing would command much admiration.

Samuel Stevenson was otherwise notable as the principal architect to the Belfast Co-operative Society, and he was responsible for the greater part of its towering range of buildings in York Street, as well as for a number of branch stores. The York Street series of buildings [31] was completed in sections during the years just before 1914; the effect of the contrasting layers of red brick and white stone is rather that of streaky bacon; a quite pleasant Ionic dome, and a variety of clocks, urns, and swags, are dumped on the roofline in an off-hand sort of way. A rather similar, but much more pleasing, use of contrasted bands of stone and brickwork may be seen in the admirable Irish National Foresters' Hall at 37 Divis Street,[32] built by J. J. Phillips in 1906.

Gradually the new styles of the new century reached Belfast. The leading practitioners of *art nouveau* seem to have been Blackwood and Jury; it was remarked that their new very ornate block of 'Carrara' artifical stone in Castle Place (1905; now much mutilated) 'breathed a nouveau siècle spirit'.[33] 'The style is of the modern moderny—L'Art Nouveau, I believe it is called, but the phrase is detestable' . . . 'The conditions of our modern shop architecture, chief of which is the necessity to impose a brick or stone building, possessing the old measure of massiveness, on top of two storeys of almost unbroken plate glass front, present a problem which would make dead-and-gone architects to turn in their graves, could they learn of it'.[34] But this firm had no objection to working in other styles: their Ballymacarrett Branch Public Library was described as 'a modern mélange of Tudor and Queen Anne'.[35] The excellent Ulster Bank branch at 151-7 Shankill Road (1903) is a fine piece of Queen Anne revival work.[36] Indeed, they even built a stockbroker's Tudor pub (now a branch of the Belfast [37] Bank) at the foot of Bradbury Place in 1912.

---

[28]   *Irish Builder*, 1900, p. 357.
[29]   Nikolaus Pevsner, *The Buildings of England: London, Vol. I, Cities of London and Westminster*, (London, 1957), p. 471.
[30]   *Irish Builder*, 1907, p. 778.
[31]   Much bombed, much altered: the most recent section at one time cladded in brown plastic like bars of chocolate, then again recladded in windowless white.
[32]   Gone.   [33]   *Irish Builder*, 1904, p. 772.
[34]   *Ibid.*, 1905, p. 341.   [35]   *Ibid.*, 1903, p. 1960.
[36]   Bombed: only the ground floor, greatly mutilated, remains standing.
[37]   Today, Northern Bank.

58

High Victorian public-house architecture is one of
the richest and most satisfying styles ever invented.
(This over-statement aroused the justifiable
derision of one reviewer of the first edition of this
work). Gin Palaces were genuinely palatial. Pl. 58:
The *Bee Hive*, 193 Falls Road, has been extensively
bomb-damaged, but the central feature shown here
survives. Pl. 59: The *Crown* Liquor Saloon was
acquired by the National Trust in 1978 and has been
extensively restored.

59

60

Pl. 60: The staircase and entrance hall to the Gasworks Offices are as ornamented, in gleaming coloured tilework, as any public house. Still intact, despite all the misfortunes which have befallen the Gasworks.

Pl. 61:: The Dunville Memorial Fountain, completed in 1892, is an equally vigorous exercise in terra-cotta.

61

62

Stairs of every kind lend themselves to exuberant treatment. The sinuous and elaborate curves of the garden staircase of Belfast Castle are exceptional; the architect of this *jeu d'esprit*, added in 1894, is unknown. Undergoing restoration. Pl. 63: The remarkable pulpit of Christ Church, College Square North, dates from the renovation of the church by William Batt in 1878. Still intact, despite the numerous bomb and arson attacks to which Christ Church has been subjected.

63

64

65

66

e front of the City Hall (Pl. 65) looks its best when
odlit; its back view down Linenhall Street (Pl. 67) is
y much more satisfactory in daylight, especially on a
nny summer morning. Pl. 64: The ponderously
ate lamp-posts, erected outside the home of the Lord
yor for the time being, seem to date from the
lding of the City Hall. Pl. 66: The Scottish Provident
titution, built in sections between 1899 and 1902,
wers massively across Donegall Square at the City
ll.

69

Pl. 68: (opposite) Sinclair Seamen's Church was turned into a kind of maritime museum by the Rev. Samuel Cochrane, BA, RN, after his installation in 1902. Pl. 69: The Ocean Buildings, completed in 1902 in a pink baronial Gothic style. Pl. 70: Ballynafeigh Methodist Church, in the 'American-Romanesque' style, built in 1899. Pl. 71: Clonard Picture House, a charming Italianate building completed in 1914: bombed, vandalised, and demolished.

70

72

Pl. 72: The memorial to the first Marquis of Dufferin, in the
grounds of the City Hall, was jointly composed by the architect
Brumwell Thomas and the sculptor Frederick Pomeroy, and
typifies the imperial pretensions of Edwardian Belfast.

There are one or two fine examples of *art nouveau* by unknown architects; the best is Crymble's music-shop [38] at 58 Wellington Place, with delightful plaque, obelisks, tracery   *
and curlicues, all with a musical flavour. Another is the Store Bar [39] in Church Lane, dating from 1905, with fine curving windows and tilework.

Not only new styles in ornament, but new means of communication, demanded expression. A wave of cinema-building swept over Belfast during the Edwardian period; and these new pleasure-halls were as anxiously ornamented to flatter their users as the Moscow Underground. Not for nothing were they called 'Picture Palaces'. Various styles were tried out by various architects; almost none survive in anything approaching their original state; but the charming Clonard Picture House [40] at 140 Falls Road (Plate 71), built by W. J. Moore in 1914, remains externally as it was: a very pleasant wide-eaved fantasy on an Italianate theme.

New housing continued to spread outwards; in 1905 an attempt was made to found a Garden Colony in Belfast. Its promoter was an estate agent, Sir Robert McConnell. His plans were ambitious, his advertisements enticing; the site, at Cliftonville Circus, was within a penny tramfare of the city's centre, in open country on the bare hillside looking upwards towards the Cave Hill and the Castle, downwards towards the Lough. The layout, by W. J. Walshe, provided for three open gardens; tree-lined roadways; a central pleasure-garden, with a tea-house, flag staff, and bandstand; no two houses in the colony were to be exactly alike.[41] The streets were to be called Aster, Begonia, Daffodil, Hollyhock, and Fern Gardens; and Sir Robert undertook to plant 100,000 shrubs, flowers and trees. The houses were to be sold at cost price—the cheapest costing £240—and the advertisements promised: 'It only costs a penny from the Junction, and you will see some of the prettiest villas that have been erected since Noah left the Ark . . . The beautiful panorama unfolded cannot be duplicated . . . Tennis Lawn for the Girls. Cricket Pitch for the Boys. Playgrounds for the children'.[42]

Unfortunately, the venture did not survive the harsh winds of economic pressure; the gardens were all built over, the tea-house and bandstand never erected; the streets more prosaically renamed. But a number of survivors of the original scheme may still be seen in the leafy streets between Westland Road and Knutsford Drive.

Indeed, there were great fluctuations in the building trade and in the general prosperity of Belfast during the years before the War. Industrial building was spasmodic. During these years, wages were low, there was much unemployment, and in consequence much economic distress, recurrent labour troubles and strikes, in which James Larkin and James Connolly took a notable part. In 1899, the *Irish Builder* had reported that 'at the end of last year 10,000 working-class houses were lying vacant due to over-development out of all proportion to the population or any probably increase'. In 1905 'the greatest depression still exists in the building trade'; but in 1910 there was 'a sudden upsurge in the Belfast building trade, resulting in a rise in brick prices of over 30 per cent'. Many factories and warehouses were built, but the highest peak of achievement was the year 1913, when the Olympic, then the largest ship in the world, was the first vessel to enter the new Thompson dry dock, designed by Redfern Kelly (the Harbour Engineer), then the largest dry dock in the world.

Middle-class houses continued to be erected without much regard for economic

38   Somewhat damaged by nearby bombs; no longer used as a music shop; but, happily, listed. Designed by W. J. W. Roome (drawings in City Hall).
39   Disappeared.   40   Bomb-damaged, then demolished.   41   *Irish Builder*, 1906, pp 360-3.
42   Scrapbook in possession of Messrs R. J. McConnell & Co., Belfast.

fluctuations. In 1911, C. F. A. Voysey designed a house for a linen merchant, Mr Robert Hetherington, at 149 Malone Road: its actual erection was supervised by Young and Mackenzie.[43] It is a pleasant two-storeyed house of white rough-cast, with sandstone trim, and Voysey's characteristic buttresses giving it a slightly pyramidal air; the interior has the disadvantage that the tops of the windows are inconveniently low, and the bottoms inconveniently high. so that one can look out in comfort neither standing up nor sitting down. The interior has been somewhat altered, but a number of original details remain; the arched fire-places, the door and window furniture, are as designed by Voysey; best of all, there is an exceptionally fine and elegant square stairwell and staircase.

Another unexpected work by an English architect of eminence is that of the young Mr A. E. Richardson, later Sir Albert Richardson, PRA, who in 1912 designed the very plain and correct plinth for the statue of Lord Kelvin in the Botanic Gardens,[44] the statue itself being by Albert Bruce-Joy. The plinth originally stood on a small grassy knoll; unfortunately the Parks authorities, in their enthusiasm for a large bed of wallflowers, have levelled the knoll away, thus revealing the fact that the stone plinth stands skew-whiff on a crumbling brick foundation.

Many churches of all denominations were built in Belfast during the years between 1900 and 1914; but very few of them were of any architectural interest or merit. The best ** ecclesiastical building of these years is certainly the Roman Catholic Church of the Holy Cross, at Ardoyne, built for the Passionist Order by the firm of Walter G. Doolin and R. M. Butler, of Dublin. It was started in 1900 and finished in 1902; while Doolin seems to have had the principal part in the original plans, he was a very old man, and died at the age of eighty-one in 1900; the plans were executed by Butler, who was solely responsible for the outside design of the Lady Chapel to the North of the nave. This is a gem, beautifully proportioned and delightfully detailed, which was an addition to the original design. As a whole, the exterior of the church is rather forbidding, a Romanesque façade flanked by two square towers with château hats perched on the shoulder of the long hill at the top of the Crumlin Road. But the inside is bright, light, gay and airy. The planked and vaulted roof is a charming powder-blue skyscape with angels, painted by one Brother Mark, assisted by 'Signor Candine of London'; there are two enormous mural paintings, thirty feet by twelve, on the chancel walls, also by Brother Mark,[45] a little soupy but not much. There is an admirable white high altar; cheerful mosaics; excellent modern electric light fittings; and a liberal use of white paint throughout (with touches of red and blue). The carving outside is by James Ovens of Dublin, inside by Messrs Jackson and Copeland, both of Belfast. Altogether, the whole church is in brisk cheerful colourful good taste—a highly satisfying departure from the usual norm of church architecture and decoration.

The same cannot be said of the Church of the Holy Redeemer, Clonard, built by J. J. McDonnell between 1907 and 1911. Though there are rather fine if incongruous modern mosaics in the arch spandrels of the nave, the lower layers of the interior are conservative and uninspired. The West façade, however, is rather splendid; a tremendous rose window gazes serenely out over a broad sloping piazza—when it is bare of parked cars.

The last twelvemonth before the outbreak of the First World War saw no radical developments in the building programme of the city. The Zoo [46] and pleasure-grounds at

43 *Irish Builder*. 1911. p. 562.
44 *Ibid.*, 1911, p. 562.   45 *Ibid.*, 1902, p. 1264.
46 Now to be resited and built anew. at great cost.

Bellevue, on the slopes of the Cave Hill, were completed (in the teeth of much criticism, and of grave difficulties with subsidence) partly to the designs of Messrs Cheal and Sons, Zoo and Park Experts, and partly to those of Mr Nance, Secretary of the Tramway Company. A competition was held for the design of the new municipal Art Gallery (largely inspired by Sir Hugh Lane): the first prize was awarded to much-criticized drawings by J. C. Wynne, of Edinburgh.[47] No less than eight Picture Palaces were started or completed. The Prudential Assurance Company erected an enormous classical office block, to designs by Paul Waterhouse, in Wellington Place (demolished in 1963). A Mrs Mary McGreavey obtained bye-law permission for the erection of a byre for her cows in Joy Street, within five hundred yards of the City Hall. The Ulster Volunteer Force, 110,000 strong, was drilling furiously. There was mutiny at the Curragh. 25,000 rifles and 2,500,000 rounds of ammunition were smuggled ashore to the Ulster Volunteers. Part of the British battle-fleet was ordered to Lamlash, just across the North Channel, perhaps to bombard Belfast. Destroyers were stationed in Bangor Bay to patrol the waters around the coast. The Home Rule Bill passed its third reading, and King George V called a conference at Buckingham Palace. There was fighting on the barricades in St Petersburg. The armies of Europe mobilized.

In the spring and early summer of 1914, passions in Belfast ran high; buildings were reduced to piles of smoking rubble; but not by the Kaiser's Zeppelins, nor by the guns of the British Fleet. Abbeylands, the Whiteabbey home of Major-General McCalmont, was burned; damage assessed at £11,000. Orlands House, former palace of the Roman Catholic Bishop, was burned; damage, £20,000. The Tea house in Bellevue Gardens was burned; damage, £1,200. Annadale Hall was set alight, but extinguished just in time. The 'handsome pavilion of the Cavehill Bowling and Tennis Club' was burned; damage £1,000.[48] 'The usual literature and feetmarks' showed that it was all the work of suffragettes.

[47]   Now the Ulster Museum, greatly enlarged and extended, 1965, to designs by Francis Pym; see David Evans, *Introduction to Modern Ulster Architecture* (UAHS, Belfast, 1977), p. 35.
[48]   *Irish Builder*, 1914, pp 263, 295; and *Belfast News Letter*, April and May 1914, *passim*

SELECT BIBLIOGRAPHY

Works published between 1966 and 1985 relating
wholly or substantially to the buildings of Belfast

Brett, C.E.B. 'The Georgian town: Belfast about 1800' and 'The Edwardian city: Belfast about 1900' in J. C. Beckett and R. E. Glasscock (eds), *Belfast: the origins and growth of an industrial city*. London, B.B.C., 1967.

Rowan, A. J. and Brett, C. E. B. *List of buildings in the vicinity of The Queen's University of Belfast*. Belfast, U.A.H.S., 1968.

Dixon, Hugh and Evans, David. Revised edition of above list. Belfast, U.A.H.S., 1975.

Brett, C. E. B., and McKinstry, Robert. *Survey of the Joy Street and Hamilton Street district of Belfast*. Belfast, U.A.H.S., 1971.

McCracken, Eileen. *The Palm House and Botanic Gardens, Belfast*. Belfast, U.A.H.S., 1971.

Brett, C. E. B. *Court Houses and Market Houses of the Province of Ulster*. Belfast, U.A.H.S., 1973.

Dixon, Hugh. *An Introduction to Ulster Architecture*. Belfast, U.A.H.S., 1975.

Brett, C. E. B. *Roger Mulholland, Architect, of Belfast*. Belfast, U.A.H.S., 1976.

Dixon, Hugh. *Soane and the Belfast Academical Institution*. Dublin, 1976.

Evans, David. *An Introduction to Modern Ulster Architecture*. Belfast, U.A.H.S., 1977.

Maguire, W. A., Dixon, Hugh and Wallace, Craig. *Malone House*. Belfast, U.A.H.S., 1983.

Walker, B. M. and Dixon, Hugh. *No mean city: Belfast 1880-1914 in the photographs of Robert French*. Belfast, Friar's Bush Press, 1983.

Walker, B. M. and Dixon, Hugh. *In Belfast town: early photographs from the Lawrence collection, 1860-1880*. Belfast, Friar's Bush Press, 1984.

Pierce, Richard and Coey, Alastair. *Taken for Granted*. Belfast, R.S.U.A./H.B.C., 1984.

ABBREVIATIONS

B.B.C.	British Broadcasting Corporation
H.B.C.	Historic Buildings Commission
P.R.O.	Public Records Office, London
P.R.O.N.I.	Public Record Office of Northern Ireland
R.S.U.A.	Royal Society of Ulster Architects
U.A.H.S.	Ulster Architectural Heritage Society

INDEX

This Index may be employed as a Guide to buildings of interest in Belfast by reference to the names of streets which are printed in capital letters.

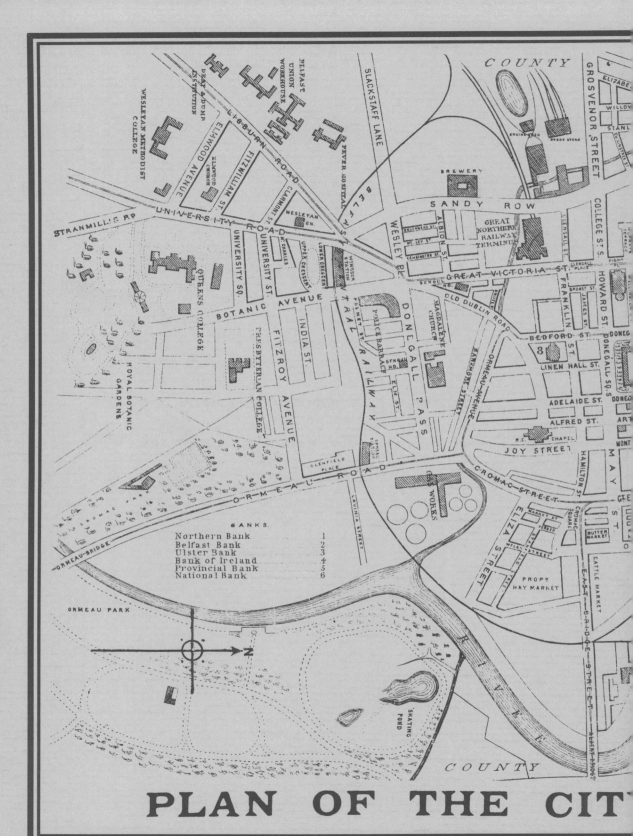

PLAN OF THE CIT

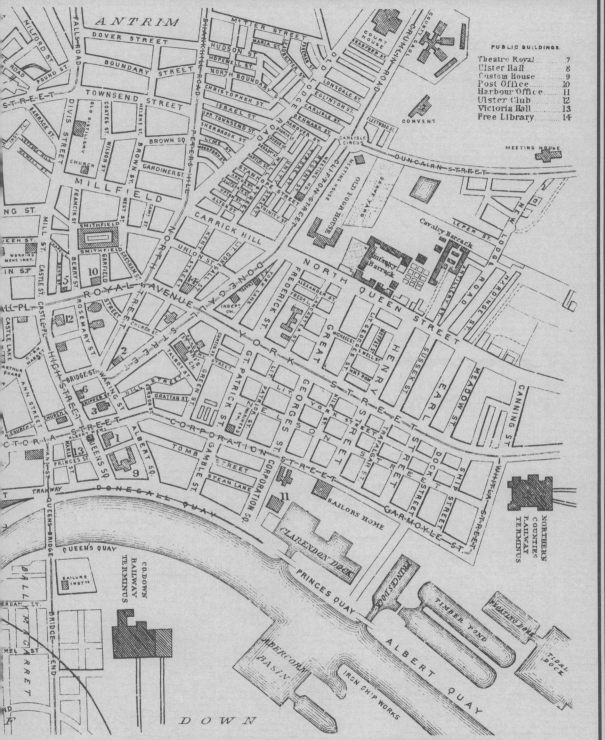

PUBLIC BUILDINGS.

Theatre Royal	7
Ulster Hall	8
Custom House	9
Post Office	10
Harbour Office	11
Ulster Club	12
Victoria Hall	13
Free Library	14

OF BELFAST 1897